CW01023886

THE
ANGLE
OF THE
CAST

GWILYM HUGHES

1

The Angle of the Cast
First Edition August 2009

Published by G.H. Sporting
Tel: 01490 412731
Email: ghughes2@btinternet.com

Set in Book Antiqua

The events and opinions in this book originate from the author. The publisher accepts no responsibility for their accuracy.

Printed and bound in Great Britain by Orphans Press Ltd., Leominster.

THE ANGLE OF THE CAST

As a boy, the two loves of my life were fishing and rugby. The story is written on my rugby career but thankfully I am still fishing and enjoying it more than ever. It is also less demanding on the old body!

There are however fishermen and fishermen. Some have that special something that implies a form of understanding and skill well beyond normal anglers.

One such exceptionally gifted angler is Gwilym Hughes. I first met him many years ago when I was involved in making some fishing programmes in Welsh for the BBC. We have been friends ever since. Gwilym started fishing whilst he was at School and, like myself with rugby, he admits that little did he think as he walked to the river with his rod and worms that one day he would reach the pinnacle of achievement within the fine art of 'Fly fishing'.

Gwilym was first capped for Wales in 1983 and soon reached the top of his game coming away from Loch Harray in Orkney with the coveted 'Brown Bowl' trophy for the top rod in that particular International match. Fifteen years later in 1998 Gwilym did the 'double', walking away from the River Tweed in Scotland with the 'Moc Morgan' trophy for the top rod in the River's International Match. This marked a historic moment within the home International Fly fishing scene as he became the first angler ever to have won both titles of 'Lake and River International Champion'.

Over his career many more awards and prizes have come his way, including his induction into the prestigious 'Hardy Hall of Fame'.

Over the years I have been an avid reader of articles that Gwilym has published in various angling journals, always hugely knowledgeable but importantly you could go out and do what he suggested and see results coming quickly.

All this knowledge, skill and experience have now come together in this book about his life within the 'Angling' game. There is insight on every page - from the memory of his very first trout, boyish adventures and hilarious incidents, through the stages of learning and development of skills in angling to the fulfilment and elation of reaching International status. From all this comes a good read and an angling bible.

Gwilym might very well have set about his 'Fly fishing' as I set about my 'Rugby' trying to harness his natural skills and adapting them to the challenges at hand. He has covered every aspect of this remarkable angling progress with some original, thought provoking and simple-to-follow guidance. This book can only enhance one's angling experience.

Gareth Edwards CBE

INTRODUCTION

Why write a book about my life in general and its connection through to 'Angling'? The reasons are many and varied and I cannot exactly say that one would take priority over another, whereas collectively it would make sense to say that 'Angling' is my life and always has been. Other matters within my life have quite often taken second place, such has been and still remains the grip of its addictiveness. I have set out to record memories of my experiences in the hope that one day someone may find them useful. The dedication within is directed at my parents, Ella and Griff who were doubtless bewildered by how their little boy evolved through time. It is also dedicated to my wife Sarah who understands me totally, cares for me, and allows me the time and space to be who I am. Last but not least, my children Jenifer and Heather who often wondered where their father was when he was not in work.

My thanks go out to everyone with whom I have had the pleasure of their company. Their advice, be it good or bad, has helped shape the character that will appear in the following pages.

I will do my utmost to avoid areas that I believe are adequately covered in other fishing publications but, in case if I do transgress I apologise to all you splendid authors now.
As advice goes, and for what it's worth, always listen to others. It is the lessons from their experiences that will allow you to gain your own, easier and quicker, thus affording you more knowledge and time to exploit your own chances in angling. Try, though it be not easy at times, to be at peace with everyone and, whatever you do, don't waste too much time reading this when you could be fishing, leave it for those moments when you can't.

Gwilym Hughes

Steve,

May your line always
be tighter than mine!

Simon

Sowing the fishing seed

So where did it all begin then? The phrase 'knee high to a grasshopper' seems to fit because I had to hold onto the edge of the draining board alongside the kitchen sink and pull myself up to peep over at the display of the catch from the night before. Sometimes there were up to a dozen or so, bars of silver, laid out alongside each other, some going the whole length of the draining board with their tails hanging over the sink area, I would run my finger along their sides and scales would come off easily, like miniature five pence pieces, and then that addictive scent on my finger, I used to climb onto a stool so I could look into their eyes and wondered if they could see me. Whilst some children used blocks to learn to count, I was blessed with counting the number of sea trout on the draining board.

Sea trout, Brown Trout and Salmon abounded in three rivers not more than a half hour bicycle ride away from my home, the Dwyfawr, Dwyfach and Erch. My father used to cycle to work and to his fishing, hard days by comparison to the modern time. The tiled living room floor had square coco matting covering in front of the fireplace and my mother used to empty the used wet tea leaves from the teapot along one side of the mat and brush them with a small hand brush all the way along to the other side. They were good at picking up every bit of dust. That mat was hard on the knees and if I sat on it for any length of time it would leave indentation patterns on my legs, as short trousers were the order of the day.

Then she would collect it onto a small shovel and throw it on the open fire. There was always a coal fire as the oven was alongside and I can remember well the fine meals and the rice puddings that came out of it.

Fish caught were eaten, shared out between family and friends and the surplus sold on to the fishmongers in Pwllheli and Criccieth. Some also went to the hotels and guesthouses. In those days there was no supermarket to buy fish from, and it was a form of income in support of the main wage to supplement the family. Fishing was therefore both a godsend and a source of pleasure, thrown into one, the enjoyment in the catching and eating and the few shillings of extra income in the bargain.

'Rhydygwystyl Creameries' collected milk produced in the farms on the Lleyn Peninsula and Eifionydd and my father used to drive a milk tanker delivering that milk to various dairies. I recall journeys to Whitchurch, Liverpool, Wrexham, Tarvin, and used to accompany him on some. They were real adventures as the trip started in the middle of the night and at a maximum speed of 30mph, the noisy diesel Foden tanker bearing the number 3 took quite a few hours to cover the 100 or so miles. The seating position was high up and I could see out over the hedges and marvel at the beauty of the Countryside, especially so the rivers and brooks through Snowdonia.

It was on one of those return journeys from Whitchurch that I recall my father stopping in Bangor on Dee in a fishing tackle shop and purchasing a second hand 'Young's' Pridex Salmon Reel bearing a Double Tapered silk line. In my mind's eye I recall walking into the shop off the street, there was a room to the left and another to the right off a corridor and I recall him pointing out to me marks made on the wall within the shop to show the height of the water as and when the nearby River Dee burst its banks. This was way before the time of the Tryweryn and Brenig Dams. Whilst my father negotiated a deal - I believe that it cost him five pounds, almost half a week's wages - I was invited into the room on the right where I watched, mesmerised, by a lady sat at a table dressing a built wing Salmon Fly. There were a number of similar finished flys on the table miniature masterpieces. We were not there long enough and I just didn't want to leave. I'll never forget it.

That very same reel fifty or so years on is still with us today and I bore witness to many a screeching battle in my childhood and youth as I accompanied my father on forays in the upper reaches of the River Dwyfawr in pursuit of Salmon and Sea trout when the river was in flood. The rod it was attached to was acquired from an angler who lived close to my home, the late Rhys Price Jones, who later introduced me to lake fishing. It was a three-piece 14' green heart, if memory serves me right. My father accidentally broke the top section whilst out fishing one day and replaced it with a solid fibreglass piece – this was in the days preceding the availability of hollow fibreglass.

He also had a spinning rod made out of a metal tank aerial fitted with a fixed spool reel. The way tackle and methods have evolved over a period of 50 years is mind-boggling. At the same time the demise of the Salmon and Sea trout stocks for various reasons has also caused great concern, and quite rightly so. My grandson will not have imprinted in his mind's eye in his early years fish stocks of the proportions that I saw at his age. Now, whilst this saddens and worries me, the passing of time inevitably brings with it new experiences and unforeseen outcomes, I suppose that's life and we have to live with it, or do we. Is it not our duty to ensure that there is something left for those that follow us?

When I was about five years of age my farther became the proud owner of a Triumph Speed Twin Motor Cycle, 500cc, maroon in colour. After that travelling about became easier and more distant fishing forays became more frequent. Initially when I sat behind him on the motorcycle I remember my mother strapping me on with a belt around my waist and my father's waist in case her little boy fell off the back. Not that my father was a careless rider, it was a case of the telegraph posts on the side of the roads looking as close to each other as the teeth on a comb, by comparison to the days I had sat side saddle on the crossbar of his pushbike. There was no lawful requirement in those days to wear a crash helmet and my father had a leather peaked cap, motor cycle glasses and large leather gauntlets - well they seemed large for me because when the motor cycle was not in use I would dress up in them and sit astride the machine on its stand alongside the house, making revving noises and the like. Most of all I recall holding on very tightly when we went anywhere.

Having watched my father fishing with a worm in a flood for Salmon (plate 1) and catching a fair few and also Sea trout, the 14' green heart would be used with the Young's reel and the fly line. At the business end a cast made up of about a yard of 12lb to 15lb nylon with four or five lead shots thereon about eight inches away from quite a large hook, which was dressed with two blackhead worms completely covering the hook. The worms would be placed, not cast, into an eddy or slack water behind a rock and trotted downstream with the lead weight keeping them near the river bed on gravely areas where the fish rested up from the rushing flood water. Over a period of time one would learn the best taking areas on certain heights of water, although that changed every so often as the riverbed shifted under the extreme water pressure of large floods. Using the 'fly' rod for worming? There was method in the madness so to speak as one would be moving constantly from pool to pool and as the water became clearer and the flood water start to recede the fish would move out into streamy areas. Then, all my father had to do was to change casts and he would be fishing the fly in some pools casting in the traditional overhead method and quickly changing back again to a worm in another as we moved on. This art practiced by my father was self-taught as my grandfather was not an angler. Those thoughts of the past and the rapid learning curve that ensued brings back a memory that will stay with me.

Ifan , my cousin, who was a few years older than I, was on holiday with us during the summer school holidays. It had rained heavily in the night and there was a big golden-brown flood in the small river 'Wen' that runs through the village of Chwilog, near to my home. My adventures and escapades had taken me along its banks several times whilst out with my friends and I had on numerous occasions surveyed the brown trout in some of the pools, off bridges and high banks. In those days, shoals of them fed avidly on insects floating downstream. Whilst I had never been allowed out alone to fish, I had watched the older lads from the village try their hand at it, with some success I may add, but only when the water was high after heavy rain. In low water however the trout would disperse immediately on approach and park themselves under stones and overgrown banks - their escape from the approaching danger.

We had been to the village shop for some items of groceries for my mother when I met one of the local lads on his way to the river. After a brief discussion, we returned the groceries home and I asked my mother if I could take Ifan to the river fishing - my plan was that we could borrow my father's tank aerial rod and maybe catch some trout for tea. My mother did not approve, as she knew well that I could not be trusted at such a tender age with the metal rod and furthermore she was pretty certain that my father possibly would also not approve.

My mother read the disappointment in my face and alleviated the developing situation by taking us out to the nearby field and cutting from a thicket, a thin hazel stick that was almost straight and quite flexible about six feet in length. She proceeded to strip the bark off with a knife and set about with a pair of pliers breaking and bending safety pins and attaching them to the hazel stick with some black insulating tape to create rings for the line to run through. A small silvery coloured metal fishing reel was found in a drawer and attached to the thicker end of the stick in the same manner, followed by cutting a long piece of white string, which she wound onto the reel as the main line. The string was threaded through the safety pin rings she had created. My father's fishing bag was raided and some nylon, lead weights and a hook secured to complete the outfit. The connecting knots were of the multiple overhand type. It was a kind of roles reversed whilst I dug the garden and Ifan collected the worms into a clean jam jar, usually it was I who collected them for my father as he dug. We had created a handle for the jar with some string whilst my mother had been busy at the rod building exercise.

We set off through the village towards the river and there couldn't have been prouder lads in wellingtons in the whole of Wales that day. Ifan carried the worms and I carried the rod and we negotiated a deal whereby we would take it in turns to catch the trout. My mind was racing with visions of a draining board full of fat golden-bellied beauties to await my father's arrival home from work.

We arrived at a location on the river just below a railway bridge near to 'Plas' farm about half a mile upstream from the village. The warm sun shone through the trees and glistened in the boiling current of the swollen stream. The scent from the drying out marsh lingered in my nostrils and is still with me now. I showed Ifan how to dress the hook with the worm, it was my go first and I dropped the worm into the eddy at the side of the current and immediately felt some fierce tugging at the end of my very own fishing rod. In my excitement I lifted immediately and to my disappointment there was no fish and most of the worm had gone.

Ifan's turn was next and he experienced the same problem - the educated trout were cunningly removing the worm off the hook. Well, it was either their cunning or perhaps our inexperience in the matter at hand that was the problem! We paused for a moment and watched a steam-train roll by with a couple of carriages and about a dozen goods carriages behind little realising that that image would be imprinted on my mind for ever.

As I threaded the next worm onto the small hook I decided to lift hard into the first pull, manoeuvring the worm out alongside the current. The line tightened and I gave an almighty heave and saw a small trout fly out of the river over my head, parting company with the business end worm and hook and drop off into the marsh behind, I was onto it in a flash - I suppose that the commotion could be likened to a cat attacking a mouse in long grass. The trout was finally in my grasp and almost speechless with excitement and shaking from the adrenalin rush, I shot off for home like a bolting rabbit in front of a spaniel, leaving poor

Ifan to carry the rod and worm jar following on. I suppose I could claim the fastest half-mile in outsize wellingtons ever covered, for when I reached the back door I was completely out of breath. I produced the fish for mother - it could not have been more than five inches long. I had held it so tight in the palm of my hand that the flanks had dried out and crinkled up in the heat and my mother prised my hand open, finger by finger. She held the small trout under the cold-water tap and placed it on the draining board. Proudly I was up on the stool examining the catch when Ifan arrived at the back door.

My memory fades a little following that point in that momen tous day's events and for fear of using imagination rather than memory, I'll leave it there. I was so proud of its perfect beauty regardless of size or numbers—gone had the thoughts of a draining board full of spotted fin perfect golden bellies. I had just learnt from that first time experience that there was a little more skill and knowledge involved in the art of successfully catching and landing that trout than there was in just venturing out in its pursuit. This was a key lesson in my angling development.

Whilst my father praised my success he also scolded me for bringing such a small fish home, I was told that they had to be at least 7" long or the bailiff would take me to court. Whilst I did not realise it at the time that I was under the age of the re-sponsibility required in law for prosecution, the message served it's purpose It did not prove necessary to tell me twice.

Home, Tackle, my first Sea trout
and some tales

It was the marriage of the broad picture of trial and error and watching closely every move my father made and listening carefully to his advice that enhanced my knowledge in those early years. I was eight years old and recall as if it was yesterday a fierce flood in the river Dwyfawr, it had broken out into the fields in many places leaving large pools in any crevasse. My father was at work and when he arrived home at lunchtime, he told me we would go fishing. Excitement in the extreme, difficult to describe in words - the tackle was gathered together and he dug for worms in the garden whilst I gathered them up into a tin, as they appeared. Strange though it may seem, the roles were reversed when Ifan was involved prior to the excursion onto the River Wen and that first trout, I had the experience and good fortune of having watched my father dig for worms, therefore I could show him how. My mother made us a quick lunch, with a warning to be home by six o clock. The Triumph speed twin was soon on the road and I carried the rod bags under one arm and held on with the other. Only a five minute or so ride and we were in the upper reaches of the River Dwyfawr, parking in the farmyard at Ty Cerrig ready to walk downstream. I recall my father speaking to the farmer at Ty Cerrig who produced a Salmon of about six pounds he'd caught that morning. I can see him now - he had a mop of very white hair and only one eye. My father told me that he'd suffered some accident or other. However he was a great fisher and kind gentleman, giving my father a salmon fly, a sure fire killer of fish and wished us luck as we parted company. I can remember inspecting the pattern tied on a size 6 hook. The body of the fly was red wool with a gold twist and brown hackle. (Plate 3)

The journey downstream from pool to pool was not an easy one for me and my short legs as we walked through very wet boggy areas that was strewn with briars, reeds and rocks with deep holes where the cattle's hoofs had sunk in the soft ground. The river was accessible only at certain points due to what seemed to my eight year old eyes impenetrable thickets of hazel trees and willow bushes which one had to push through. Such was my enthusiasm however, that it mattered not. The river was fining off and some of the usual taking spots did not hold fish, so a few changes were made from worm to fly and vice versa as we worked our way downstream.

We came to a part of the river just below some exceptionally rough water above a pool that carries the name 'Allt Goch' (Red Hill) where there is a glide in-between some large boulders and a willow tree covers half of the river with the branches reaching right into the water. This was a great lie for fish. My father changed to the fly and placed the 'killer' fly given to him earlier on the dropper, with a Blue Charm on the point. A cast aimed at the far bank saw the flies sweep round through the fast current into the eddy and as sweet as anything a fish head and tailed on it. I saw it clearly, but it did not connect. My father immediately told me he had been standing in the wrong place and that the fly had swept through the eddy too quickly. So he moved a couple of feet and on the second cast was into a lively sea trout that gave an excellent account of itself, jumping and cascading around the pool, the greenheart bent over almost double. The fish when tired was slid over the grassy edge of the river where the water broke over into the meadow. My father pounced on it and carried it into the marsh to deal with away from the river's edge, it was a bar of silver straight off the tide with sea lice on it a fish of four or five pounds. This was the kind of water required to fish the upper reaches, when the river was full to the brim and breaking over the grassy bank. The 'Iar Goch' (Red Hen) had worked. (Page 205)

I remember setting about trying to remove the sea lice but the blighters held on tightly and I was told off, for handling the fish too much so I left them where they were. We moved on downstream and another sea trout of about two pound was banked on a worm in 'Allt Goch'. The next pool down was 'Llyn Gwragedd' (Widow's Pool) and we were on the outside bend in the river. My father set up the spinning rod and proceeded to step onto a rock in the river. He told me that the height was right to spin that pool when the stone was starting to come into view as the flood water dropped. I climbed onto a very large rock, further upstream and watched out for fish showing themselves. It was then that an angler appeared from downstream and as he did my father hooked into a Salmon. The Angler put down his rod and bag and produced a gaff ready to assist. I re positioned myself right behind them and sat on the grass bank watching the proceedings, I clearly recall the fish going round and round the pool with the tank aerial conversion arched over, the fish jumped ever so high out of the water at times. It must have been three times the size of the larger of the two sea trout we already had and I remember also the very deep blue back contrasting with its silver flanks.

After what appeared to be an age, I shouted to my father, I had to shout for him to hear me above the roar of the flood in the river, "Dad! Dad!", "What?", "Are you going to be long?", at that very point the fish pulled free of the small spoon, the hooks came back with one straightened out. Well, if looks could kill I would not have been here to tell the tale. He never said a word and to this day I wished I hadn't said anything, but there you go. I knew I had to be back by six o clock because it was my first music / piano lesson in the village 'EGBDF', 'FACE' an all that. You had to be eight years old before the music teacher would take you on. The 'Speed Twin' had me back on time , and the fishing seed was well and truly sown within me. EGBDF indeed…**Every good boy deserves fishing**!. The fishing lesson here stands more vivid in my mind than the piano keyboard and has saved the day on many an outing, move your feet into the right position and get the angle of the cast right.

It was in 1956 or 1957 that my father first paid my subscription to the local Criccieth, Llanystumdwy and District Angling Association as a junior member – which means that I have now been a member for the past half a century. My basic angling skills were honed on the river Dwyfawr and Wen and also on the Erch in pursuit of Brown Trout, Sea trout and Salmon.

During those early years, juniors were not allowed on Association water after dark and I think that rule still persists apart from a couple of nights in a season where the full members take juniors out in search of sea trout. However a tidal section of the river below where the Dwyfawr and Dwyfach meet, roughly half a mile above the sea did not belong to the Association and therefore I was allowed to fish in this section with my father at night, although that did not really start until I was eleven years of age. There were a number of pools, Junction, Concrete, Llyn Bach (Small Pool) and another Allt Goch (Red Hill). Bont Lein (Railway bridge pool) had great holding areas for Sea trout and Salmon running in off the tides and, as the Dwyfawr and Dwyfach were spate rivers, these fish stayed in those pools for about another half a mile upstream until fresh water encouraged them to run through to the upper reaches.

Daytime fishing was not as productive although some persisted and were rewarded on light tackle and a single maggot or a small brandling worm, ledgered or float fished. At night however great catches could be made from dusk through to the dawn, using fly, fly and maggot and also worm fishing. This was mainly for sea trout as few Salmon came to this method in low water conditions. I also remember at this time having the advantage of watching some visiting anglers using a centre pin reel and very light tackle under a float with a single maggot to devastating effect on school sea trout. I was very much the 'twenty questions' boy whenever I saw something new or something I did not understand.

Half a century later, I was talking to the late Ken Smith who was the Chairman of the 'Game Angling Instructors Association', known to most as 'Smith the Fly' when he told me that he'd fished the Dwyfawr back in those days of my youth, together with a friend of his from Derby. I had some recollection that one of those visiting anglers that I watched with a Centre pin reel was a Chemist from Derby or Nottingham area and wondered if the other may have been 'Smith the Fly'. Since there was every likelihood that it was, I mentioned it but he could not recall. I am happy with the thought that it could have been him and that our paths could have crossed like this.

What he could remember however was how to use a centre-pin reel and I was privileged to get a lesson, in this art from him in his 80th year. I must say he was still exceptionally good at it. A few days later, in the post I had a surprise gift - one of his centre pin reels, It was a haunting moment when I opened the small parcel since I wondered if this was the very reel that I had seen him use all those years ago. It's a very small world really, especially so in Angling. Looking back now, I am grateful to all those who took time to explain and show me the various methods which were to prove so very useful when I enhanced and expanded my own skills.

My recollection of the early tackle I used for trouting in the river Wen and Erch whilst I was nine, ten, eleven, evades me, but I think that it was a small split cane butt section with a solid glass tip section about 9 ft in length and a black coloured spinning type fixed spool reel. Using that or something similar allowed me to hone my worming skills in a flood for trout and fine baskets of trout were carried home on a regular basis. They were all, without fail, eaten and shared among family and friends. People were always grateful for fresh, wild brown trout.

One day, whilst fishing the lower reaches of the river Dwyfawr, my father met with an Irish gentleman, Jim Sullivan, then living in Manchester. He was holidaying in the area and after a short period of time they became great friends and started fishing together at night for the fabled sea trout. Mr Sullivan used to come and stay at our house and I remember his Humber Hawk motor vehicle with large leather seats and a window separating the front and back seats.

I recall him bringing his family to stay in North Wales for a week, staying at Llanbedrog. He had his wife and five sons with him and my mother could not accommodate them all. He spoke to my father about fishing some small lakes visible from the main road between Llanystumdwy and Afonwen on Glanllynau farm. The lakes contained Rudd. He said it was a good idea for an outing with his sons and asked if I would like to go along, Although I'd never seen one, I accepted and he threw a challenge, half a crown (in those days) to the first one that caught a fish, I was into a small Rudd on the first cast, (plate1) he paid up and congratulated me. I'd never had so much money at once and perhaps a small competitive fingerprint was laid upon me that day which grew and grew into other things – but more of that later.

As time progressed so did the quality of life within the home. The Radio was exchanged for a television, an electric cooker had appeared and a fridge and a new carpet covered the living room floor, wall to wall. It was bliss on the legs.

My mother had gone out to work at the local Laundry and the income was saved to enhance the family's lifestyle. I had also become the owner of a small kitten aptly named 'Ginger' (Page 26) and we became close friends. I would have great games of marbles with 'Ginger' in the living room on the new carpet - she was an exceptional goalkeeper.

Now when the aforementioned Mr Sullivan came to stay, he would keep his fishing tackle in the umbrella section of the hallstand and I recall admiring Hardy Rods and Perfect Reels. These were properly balanced outfits and he took time to explain their uses to me. There were also a great variety of fly boxes stuffed with creations of all colours of which, in his kindness, he parted company with - a number of flies, nylon, weights, hooks and some of the quill minnow's that became a favourite lure of mine.

Whilst I never saw anyone fish with quill minnows, I personally through question and answer to Jim Sullivan and my father learnt the art, putting the advice to practice on a trial and error basis, needless to say initially my attempts at accuracy in and amongst the tree strewn banks of the River Wen met with a few disasters and it was a case of collecting the quills after the water had dropped away from various trees. These I kept in a modified biscuit tin fitted out with thin rubber foam, glued to the base.

My father started to take me night-time Sea trout fishing and just on the dusk he would allow me to fish with his rod on the run into the upper part of the Concrete pool. His set up was a double tapered silk line which would sink slowly with a cast of 8lb line about eight feet in length with two size eight flies - a Mallard Blue and Silver on the point and a Mallard and Claret on the dropper. The rod used was a 12 ft long split cane.

It turned out to be quite a few nights before I finally succeeded in connecting with that most elusive of fish. No sooner had the flies been cast across the run when a 'Sea trout' engulfed the Mallard and Claret and gave a very good account of itself for its pound weight. It was not so much the fight however but that magical take in the half light that has never left me, and possibly was the driving force of wanting more of the same experience over and over again.

I kept on going to the River with my father at night during school holidays and my main job was to guard the catch on the bank. The place was infested with rats, possibly water rats, and they'd be in your bag and away with your catch in seconds.

How fortunate I was during this time to be constantly instructed about lies and taking points, methods to adapt in different areas of the pool, the use of certain retrieves and not to retrieve very often, how to minimise the use of the flash lamp, how to note landmarks at certain taking spots, what angle to cast at and what angle to hold the rod at, and more importantly where to stand to angle the cast. It was a very big learning curve in a short space of time, but something that has stuck with me throughout my angling life especially when I now visit a new venue with all this in my mind whilst I prepare and execute my approach.

You may ask yourself, "What's all this about?" and I can only reply in one way, if you regulate your approach and analyse until you succeed you will enhance your skills at each visit. You can rely on the fact that not one visit will be the same as the last you made, and it's only through the mental logging of your experience of circumstances that prevail that those skills will be honed.

Schooling was at Chwilog Primary where most of the lessons were conducted through the medium of Welsh. However, my father ensured I learnt a new English word from a dictionary on a daily basis and when I went off at the ripe age of eleven to try the eleven plus at the secondary school in Pwllheli, part of the examination was to write an essay in English. The array of topics provided in the choice that allowed me to impart some of my experience in fishing and I still believe that the extra preparation at home resulted in the pass that I longed for, the word 'occasionally' which I had learnt was used in the essay about my participation in the art of angling. It was apt at the time as I remembered how to spell it, although it was somewhat a white lie, constant would have better described my participation but the word occasionally sounded better. Either the assessor who marked the paper was impressed or was an angler! There was a promise of a brand new bike and this did indeed appear the day after I announced that I had been successful in gaining a place at Pwllheli Grammar School. It was a metallic red coloured 'Raleigh Trent Tourist' with white plastic mudguards and straight handlebars. At last, I was independent and allowed to roam further afield. I had my very own set of wheels!

My father had sold the Triumph Speed Twin and replaced it with an Austin A35 Van with side windows in - then changed again for an Austin A40 hatchback in sky blue. I believe that this was the vehicle my mother passed her driving test in and through those learning days I was parked in the rear seat together with 'Lassie' my Cocker Spaniel (Page 26) listening to it all. Enough said about the driving lessons but it does bring back memories of Sunday afternoon rituals and some sea fishing but more of that later.

My development within angling had taken me from worming to using a quill minnow for the trout in the local river and during that very same period my music lessons had resulted in some certificates, my ability at reciting welsh poetry received awards at local and county based 'Eisteddfods' (Competitions) and also singing welsh folk songs had received similar awards. As with all good Welsh boys I was also a member of the local mixed choir - so it was not all fishing and nothing else. I had a variety of interests and these were good for personal development. A Welsh upbringing with a mixture of culture, music, sport, chapel and education was a solid start to any life.

However, despite it all there was that magic pull from the river and I practiced with the spinning rod in the back garden casting at plant pots at various distances with a small lead weight, eventually becoming very accurate. I needed to, for my initial attempts left the offering in the trees more often than not. One afternoon's casting practice brings back clearly an event I'm never likely to forget. There was an almighty bang and I recall ducking in the garden thinking someone had fired a gun at me. When I looked back towards the house I could see the kitchen window covered in a deep red, blood- like substance flowing slowly down the window. In my panic I dropped the rod and ran to the open back door to view my mother, the cat and the entire ceiling and kitchen walls seemingly covered in blood. I really thought someone had been shot and the expression on my face must have said it all because my mother who looked as bewildered as the cat , rose to her full and somewhat rosy height five feet and six inches and proclaimed indignantly that the pressure cooker had exploded on the electric ring whilst cooking the beetroot. Amongst the new gadgets at home my mother had become the proud owner of a 'Pressure Cooker' with which she could cook a meal in quick time - the contraption hissing away on the cooker. 'Ginger' (Page 26) the cat was none too pleased when my mother started using it. Unbeknown to me at the time whilst engrossed at the casting practice my father picked some beetroot and produced them at the back door for my mother to cook, before he went off somewhere in the car. The normal process would be to boil but my mother had other idea's to cook in quick time under pressure. It seems as if a piece of beetroot skin had detached itself in the cooking process and blocked the rubber valve and the pressure was so intense that the valve left its slot and embedded in the ceiling, followed in rapid succession by what appeared to be half a ton of mangled beetroot. What a mess there was with the whole place having to be redecorated and, I seem to recall, her hearing wasn't right for a week or so. Young Ginger was pretty upset by it too and I know for a fact that after that event whenever the pressure cooker came out of the cupboard 'Ginger' made herself scarce. Ever tried sponging down hot sticky beetroot pulp off a cat with warm soapy water, well it's a somewhat scratchy affair especially in short trousers!

1957 my mother 'Ella' with a 9lb Salmon
caught on the River Dwyfawr (page 47)

Aged 9 years in 1957
Chwilog Primary School

Full Rain Kit holding a 'Rudd'
at Glanllynau Lake (Page 18)

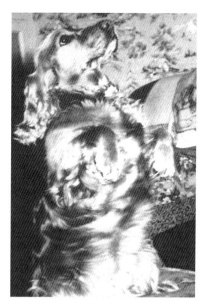

Lassie
The 'English' Dog (Page 21, 34, 35, 44)

Ginger
before the beetroot incident (Page 19, 22)

My father 'Griff' fishing in a flood on
Allt Goch Pool in the Upper Dwyfawr

Many fish of this stamp 2lb 8oz were caught on fly at
night in the tidal section of the River Dwyfawr 1962

Aspirations of being 'Elvis' 1964
(Page 55)

A garden fork sharpened up and used to 'poach' Salmon
(Page 49 - 55)

The late 'Tom Jones' and I Gwynedd River Division Bailiffs 1968.
Collecting dead fish after a pollution inicident on River Ogwen
(Page 60)

My father and I in Allt Goch Pool in the lower Dwyfawr in 1956...
I recall the day well...My father had tied on a little rubber fish on the
spinning rod which had a number of hooks protruding from it...
My attempt at casting left the little fish embedded in the
back of my head!

Trout in shallow water

Fishing, a hobby, an obsession or both?

My life was modelled around fishing and it was not unknown for me to avoid going to school on some occasions such was the draw of the river and its magic. This was not a constant problem but at times it would happen to me as I needed to be alongside the river more so than in the classroom. My pleasure in those stolen days was varied in as much that I hated myself for cheating whilst on the other hand I enjoyed every minute of my time fishing, even though at times I would catch nothing. It was that sense of freedom possibly that tipped the scales in favour of the river as against academic schooling.

I did try hard to hold my concentration and complete my school work but reality prevailed I was totally hooked and although I put some time into the schoolwork it was nowhere near the effort required that would have secured some serious educational qualifications for me. I just wanted to fish and be out on the river.

On some floods I would go out on the river Wen and walk from Chwilog all the way to Llangybi Railway Station, a distance of about two miles. The river weaved through the fields either side of the railway line with bridges having been built to carry the railway line through. This made it quite easy to cross from one side of the river to the other using these bridges.

The further upstream I went the smaller the river got, but I also found that there were not as many fish of any quality upstream. In an area near to Plas farm, often I would come across a trout of 12" but in the main they were in the 7" to 9" bracket. I would cut a small branch off a tree which carried another smaller angled branch off it and I would shape it with a penknife. The caught fish would be carried on the protruding angled branch by sliding the fish onto it through the gill and out through the mouth, it was a good way of carrying the trout, they would hang side by side and could easily be admired and, if they started to dry up then all that was needed was a quick dip in the river. Of course I did not catch all the fish that attacked the worm and sometimes a trout would drop off as it was lifted out, no net was used, I was learning all the time however. I would have a visual memory stored in my mind of the pool or part of the pool where the fish had taken the worm and this gave me an added advantage. In the same way as my father knew the lies of the Salmon and Sea trout in the upper reaches of the Dwyfawr, I learnt of the lies on the Wen and when the next flood came along I would know where to look for the fish.

My father's Uncle Harri, my great uncle, who lived in the village was very fond of the trout I caught and I would call at his home on my way from the river and drop off the catch. My Auntie would get the frying pan out and set about them for my Uncle's supper and by the time that the kettle had boiled the lard would be sizzling and the trout thrown in. Uncle Harri short in stature was built like a weight lifter and always walked slowly and his movements, thoughts and speech were purposeful.

He worked out of the Co-operative's yard, delivering coal around the village and neighbouring villages on a small lorry. I recall he used to wear a vest type garment sort of front and back with side straps, made out of leather that fitted over his clothes in a way that a sleeveless pullover would. This helped protect his back as he carried the one hundredweight sacks about. The nature of his work ensured that his clothes were always covered in coal dust, his face included and he could stand still at the side of the road in a half light and it would be difficult to see him. The local lads, who were very wary of him, kept their distance, mind, they would taunt him shouting out 'Harri Ddu' directly translated 'Black Harry' or even 'Dirty Harry!' Sometimes he would do nothing about it for a number of days but eventually he would collar the ringleader and the matter amicably sorted with a huge apology or a good clip across the ear.. I saw my

Aunty come out into the back yard on many an occasion with a bowl of hot water for him to wash and shave with on his return from work, before he entered the house.

Uncle Harri enjoyed his trout supper - he must have for when he had demolished the trout he would call for a piece of bread and the frying pan and he would wipe it clean with the bread, eating everything including the grease, nothing was wasted. He would sometimes reach into his waistcoat pocket and delve into a small leather purse and give me a sixpenny piece, possibly in payment for the trout. Of course this triggered repeated visits and although sometimes he would refuse the trout, he never sent me away empty handed but would go into the garden and collect into a bag some peas or beans or even new potatoes. He insisted that I tell my father that the vegetables were much better than what my father produced. At first I thought he was serious and was worried on both fronts as to what happened if I did or didn't say what I had been directed to. Eventually I caught on that it was just a game. The trout he refused were never wasted, there were a number of calling points for me and someone in the village would be extremely grateful of a feed from the local river, proper community spirit prevailed.

I recall visiting Uncle Harri's home of an evening on a few occasions with my father and would listen intensely at the stories they retold about their youth and the past times on the Lleyn Peninsula where they both hailed from. I recall one particular story that amused me - my father's grandfather Gruffydd Jones 'Sgoldy', refrence to individuals had the name of their home attached to the christian name, must be a Welsh thing, to avoid confusion, there could well have been a number of Gruffydd Jones' on the Lleyn Peninsula, but this Gruffydd Jones , Uncle Harri's father, worked as a fireman on a steam driven motor lorry, they referred to it as the 'traction' which travelled between Sarn Meillteyrn and Pwllheli carrying produce and supplies. Just imagine a coal driven motor lorry with large solid rubber tyres, what a major traffic jam that would cause today. Gruffydd Jones was partial to pheasant meat and the journey between Sarn and

Pwllheli necessitated travelling past and through Nanhoron Estate en route. I'm not for one minute suggesting that my great grandfather was a 'poacher' through and through but possibly more of an opportunist. For this purpose he carried on the 'traction' a shotgun and shot a pheasant at the side of the road on Nanhoron Estate, obviously the property of the Squire. The gamekeeper saw this and was immediately on the telephone as the traction pulled away and reported the matter to the local policeman at Llanbedrog, a village further on towards Pwllheli. Sure enough, the Policeman was waiting at the side of the road at Llanbedrog and signalled the 'traction' to stop. This was easier said than done because the 'traction' did not have brakes like we know them today and took about fifty yards to eventually come to a standstill. As it did so Gruffydd Jones threw the pheasant and the shotgun into the fire hold securing his innocence in the matter. The Police Officer searched the vehicle to no avail and Gruffydd Jones accused the gamekeeper of lying and character assassination. The police officer had to agree and although he guessed the truth, it was a small crime and both he and Gruffydd became friends, so much so that if ever the policeman found himself in a bit of bother whilst visiting Sarn Meillteyrn, Gruffydd Jones was sent for and would physically sort the problem out in quick time. That trait carried through into Uncle Harri and I noticed it also in my father more than once.

Thinking about the Co-operative coal yard Uncle Harry worked from in the village brings back memories of Lassie my Cocker spaniel, for when the fishing season ended my father would take up the shotgun and on a Saturday afternoon when he came home from work I would be sent to the Co-operative store in the village with two shillings and would buy four 12 bore cartridges prior to embarking in pursuit of our Sunday lunch on some local farms that my father had secured shooting rights over. It could be a pheasant a mallard, a woodcock, partridge, woodpigeon or a mixture of any, Lassie hunted the hedgerows and would give prior warning of a pending flush, yip yip, she would also have the quarry at my feet in a matter of seconds and I recall taking the empty cartridge off my father and smelling the freshly fired gunpowder or cordite from within. Those memories of my earlier years are still vivid in the mind – I loved that smell!

I would be in charge of carrying the game home and whilst my father feathered the quarry I would pick the feathers and store them, the Mallard flank feathers, especially the bronze ones, the brown partridge back feathers, the pheasant neck and tail feathers, nothing was wasted. They would be turned into fishing flies during the winter months in readiness for the following fishing season. My mother made easy work dressing the birds and Sunday dinner would be a welcome and tasty affair.

Sunday afternoons were set aside for visiting family and friends around the Lleyn Peninsula and of course my mother was learning to drive whilst Lassie and I suffered in the back seat. I do recall my father and I training Lassie when she was a pup (Page 26). Biscuits would be hid in various locations in the house and Lassie soon found them, sit, stay, seek, fetch. I wonder why we used English commands when we conversed in Welsh?.

On one Sunday afternoon we called at a house in Bryncroes on the Lleyn Peninsula, 'Erw Fair', and there was a fair number of children in the family who were prepared for bed, bathed and in their pyjamas. They were ushered upstairs on our arrival. Lassie was brought into the house and biscuits were hid in various locations, you could possibly describe it as a travelling show. 'Sit' 'Stay' 'Seek' 'Fetch'. I had gone to the toilet which was upstairs on the landing and overheard the conversation amongst the younger children in their beds and their older sister whose responsibility was to bed them down for the night, "Who are they? who are they"?, in Welsh, inquisitive research and the reply will stay with me for ever, again in Welsh "I don't know who they are, they're Welsh but the dog is English".

To revisit the quill minnow method I employed on the river Wen as the water dropped and cleared following a flood requires further explanation the minnow is formulated from a goose quill - the wire mount weighted with lead and pulled into the quill prior to shaping with a pair of pliers and attaching plastic veins to create a spin and of course a swivel at the point. This was finished by a small treble at the back, sometimes a flying treble would also be employed from the front swivel as fish used to attack the lure from the side. All that was then required was to paint on a pair of eyes and colour for the back, usually a light green and some black spots. It is a devastating lure in the right hands.

My casting practice to plant pots in the back garden proved its worth as pinpoint accuracy was required to place the minnow in the right place. I would pull it through likely lies in between rocks and under trees in the small overgrown river, where the better trout would certainly have a go. By this time the tank aerial Spinning rod, which had been broken several times, had been repaired and reduced in size and placed into my ownership. It was about seven feet in length, which was just right for the method and style of fishing in the river Wen. There would be far more takes and flashes at the minnow than there would with worm fishing in the brown flood water and it became more exciting as you could watch the fish dart after the minnow as it raced through the run on the retrieve. I would not say that there was more skill involved with fishing the minnow as against the worm, the only difference being that the casting had to be very accurate with the minnow. Both are an art and both have their place in the experience of angling and I suspect that the actual sight of fish coming at the minnow and the excitement of which eventually led to my taking up the fly rod for trout. There was also of course the added element that I did not need to have a flood or dropping river in order that I could venture out.

I had watched some of the older boys from the village fish for trout with a fly just after the flood had passed and the water clear and near to normal level. They cursed me often for getting too close and I was brusquely sent away. I suspected initially that there was some secret involved that they did not wish to share with me and it was some time after that I realised that they were only annoyed because my approach might spook the trout into heading for their hidey-holes. It was not long after this that my technique with the fly also included that ambush type of slow crouched crawl using the bank side vegetation and bushes as my screen. Some casts were no more than holding the fly and pulling onto the rod to bend it. with a quick release to get the line to spring to the desired location, maybe only the rod tip was showing over the bank towards the likely area. At the business end there would be one pattern, a 'Coch-y-Bonddu' on a size 16 hook. The cast would be allowed to swing round on the run and just the same as the minnow, trout would dart towards it, some slashing at it, others turning away at the last minute and some impaling themselves upon the hook. All of it exciting stuff and memories to take away in the minds eye forever. A health and safety warning here though, if you use the cast described please ensure that you hold it with the hook point out and be very careful else it will bury itself in your finger.

In slacker water on a glide or towards the tail end of a pool, the shallower water was far more difficult to approach as the trout would often spook with just the rod tip showing. One could see the 'V' marks in the surface of the pool created as trout rushed away to safety, but this did not matter so much once the water was slightly coloured on a dropping flood. I quickly learned that different parts of any pool would fish according to differing heights of water and the fish would take up new stations at various levels. Learning and memorising this aspect was a lesson that would hold me in good stead for later in life and would ensure that I would always be able to find someone's tea or supper, including my own.

I was to learn over the years that fishing meant different things to different people and that's not a bad thing. Some ask, "what kind of people go fishing and why?" I'm not sure that it matters. I suppose that one derives pleasure out of what you do for differing reasons, What matters is factor into the equation the pleasure aspect that is derived from just being there, the music from the river bubbling along, the wildlife, birds, flowers and fauna, the scents, the scenery the secrets of nature - it all adds up together and overtakes that moment of sadness in failure to provide the 'supper'. To be consistently successful at 'catching' fish you have to learn the various methods and become fluent in how and when to implement them - that's why they call it 'fishing' and not 'catching'. This covers a multitude of variations within the scope of 'angling' which you could argue simply means 'designed for enjoyment and fulfilment'. My hobby was growing into an obsession, not only to catch fish but also to immerse myself fully within the sphere of everything that came within the fishing game.

My first real fly rod, Lobsters and Shrimps

My father set about to build a Salmon fly rod in the newly available hollow fibreglass again 14' in length, referred to as 'Yr enwair fawr' (The big rod). It was so much lighter than the greenheart, he still uses it to this day. It has seen very many floods in the upper Dwyfawr, Llyfni, Seiont, Gwyrfai, all North Wales rivers and bent over hundreds of times into Salmon and Sea trout. He also used it to great effect in the west coast of Ireland.

Shortly after this he set about building me an 11' three piece fly rod with the same material. I recall I was twelve going thirteen when I was allowed to visit the River Dwyfawr alone at night after the Sea trout, the rod gave years of faultless service as I honed my skills. I would read the tide table and be at the river at the right time to follow the tide out of the pools as the run and pull in the water re appeared, sometimes I would be alone in the area all night and other times there would be a few anglers about. I would hide my bicycle in the field and set off to catch as many Sea trout as I could carry, them days stand vivid in my memory, the pools were blue with fish, thousands of them ranging in size from a pound to five and six pounds in and among some Salmon to the teens of pounds. During daylight hours I would climb trees overlooking the pools and look for the fish below, when the light from the sun was at the right angle to allow me to view into the depths it was an amazing sight, layer upon layer of them.

I arrived at the river, late one night to follow the tide out and was sat on the sloping gravely bank alongside the wall in the Concrete pool waiting for the tide to go. It was silent although there was a decent breeze from the southwest, rustling in the trees and leaves overhead. The wind was holding the tide in longer than it should have due to its position and the timing of my arrival was possibly quarter of an hour out. It was quite odd as there was very few Sea trout jumping in the Pool or in Llyn Bach or Allt Goch below.

An owl landed alongside and above me on the concrete wall unaware of my presence and I marvelled at how quietly it had approached. It was dark but also light enough to make out the background on the opposite bank of the river. The owl left as quietly as it had arrived as I poured myself a cup of tea from the thermos flask. No sooner than I had done this than I heard a splashing noise from somewhere the other side of the concrete wall and then the noise came again this time with some groaning. The hair stood up on the back of my neck and a shiver travelled the whole length of my body as I immediately thought someone had tried to cross the river upstream, fallen in and was drowning. I was up on my feet and torch in hand went looking in the margins upstream but to no avail. , I wondered whether I'd sort of dreamed it because of the silence and wasn't convinced that was impossible. Anyway, I returned to my spot on the gravel and drank the rest of my tea, packing my flask away in the fishing bag.

A few minutes later I heard the same groaning and splashing again, this time louder and closer and I was up again and went all the way up the side of the bank with the torch to the top of the pool, wading in the shallow water. By this time the water was running quite fast, showing that the tide was leaving the pool but again I could see no sign of anyone in trouble and called out several times, "Who's there" - to no avail. I thought that maybe another angler was playing games with me, taking advantage of my inexperience and tender years, in disgust I returned to my position preparing myself to fish the tail end of the pool.

The Concrete pool was split into two halves, a large high concrete wall had been built to keep the river in its course, but several large floods over the years had taken their toll and the wall had broken off at the end about 20 feet and laid into the pool. The water had gouged a big deep hole underneath and below this wall, making it a great holding area for the running fish with the tail end being gravelly and holding a vast shoal of Sea trout. It could be fished from either bank, but I had chosen to fish under the trees, which required a side cast above the river across the body. I waded out along side the trees almost to the top of my outsized waders in readiness to fish and released the fly and started to cast. Not more than ten feet away from the middle of the deep pool, this massive beast came out of the water like a Polaris missile towering above me and falling towards me, the splash soaking me and also the wake that followed filled my waders to the brim.

Momentarily I was glued to the spot but when I gathered my senses together my feet must have dug a crevasse in the gravel as I left the pool and up the bank, in my panic. Unbeknown to me however the line had got caught up as I ran away from the river and the reel was singing away at me, I thought that the 'beast' whatever it was had hold of my flies, so I dropped the rod, to ensure a clean getaway. I must have gone fifty yards when I realised that what I had seen was not following me. That was a relief because it's difficult to run fast or for any distance in water filled waders, believe me. I stopped, got my torch and slowly and cautiously made my way back along the path, squelch, squelch, with each cautious step. Trees separated the path from the river at this point and I found my rod, picked it up and pulled hard, the 'beast' let go and I reeled the line in, keeping the torch pointed out in the direction of the pool. I realised that my cast had gone.

I wasn't brave enough to go back and decided to head for home, I could feel my heart pumping in my throat and I was very thirsty, in between that and a few sobs and tears I got my pushbike and left for home. At the top of the hill near the petrol station and the junction with the Pwllheli and Chwilog road I stopped momentarily and drank some tea. As I rode home I was wary of every shadow in the light of the weak torch, the hair was still stood up on my neck and arms when I reached the back door. My waders were dumped outside and my trousers on the kitchen floor.

I didn't wake my mother as I knew she had work in the morning and my father had already left with the milk tanker, I climbed into my bed having dried myself with the towel and still feeling the odd wave of panic and emotion creeping over me. I eventually fell asleep and awoke to my mother leaning over me with a cup of tea and promptly set about telling her the story about the 'beast'. She burst out laughing and scuffed my hair up. The postman just told her that a 'Porpoise' had come up the river the previous day on the tide after the Sea trout and got caught in one of the pools when the tide went out. I could have kicked myself.

Next night I was there again, the 'beast' had gone, I found my cast in the trees, retied it onto the line and was soon into the 'fish'. Whilst still wary of the dark I had decided that no beast was going to keep me from the sea trout run at prime time – a time I had been waiting a whole year for.

I have now found that if I am unsure of a certain noise or sudden movement, there is always an explanation. Whilst I have been frightened out of my skin several times, I've seen nothing in fifty years that eventually could not be explained.

Another adventure that I followed in the height of summer was accompanying my father in search of Lobster amongst the rocks on the beach near to the estuary of the River Dwyfawr, my father would read the Tide table and on certain tides he would go, he was equipped with a long metal hook and an old army bag on his back, he would also carry a wide rimmed net. He would wade out dressed in boots and a bathing costume, oh, and Polaroid glasses, into the bay alongside a rocky peninsula sometimes as deep as his chest and go about the rocks prodding, the lobster would come out backwards from its hideaway, my father would carefully place the net behind it and then take the hook forward towards him, inevitably the lobster swam back into the net and was lifted out and bagged, many a fine meal was experienced. When I got bored watching, I would find an old tin on the beach and go about the pools between the rocks which the tide had left accessible and catch shrimp some as big as two inches long, I would spot the shrimp and place my hand in the water slowly taking it forward towards my quarry, the shrimp would, move and bring its feelers around onto my finger, I would bring my thumb down onto my finger slowly trapping the shrimp by the feeler, if you moved too quickly the shrimp would dart away backwards and the proceedings would have to be repeated, I'd get quite a catch maybe up to twenty or so which I would take home in the tin for my mother to boil alongside the lobsters my father caught., or taken to Doctor Prydderch's surgery in Criccieth, he used them to fish for Salmon on the River Glaslyn.

The sea levels are rising at an alarming rate; some productive rocks that used to be accessible twenty years ago cannot now be approached in the same manner, also there is a serious decline in the shrimp and blue crab population also the winkles that provided another type of feed now and again, the lugworm banks have also diminished and are a mere shadow of what they used to be, is this the sign of a lack of food in the ocean in that area, I wonder.

So it was all systems go at that time and I would go fishing on dusk or to suit the times of the tide, sometimes getting up in the middle of the night and cycling down to the river, and follow the tide out of the pools on the ebb, I'd more often than not have the place to myself, I wasn't scared to be out there alone. As I explained whilst many occurrences frightened the life out of me during those early years it never broke my enthusiasm for that Sea trout magic.

Introduction to Lake fishing
and my first Salmon

Rhys Price Jones lived no further than a stone's throw away
from my home. He was a kind and quiet gentleman and a keen
angler - member of the Criccieth Llanystumdwy and District
Angling Association Committee. I would see Mr Jones quite
often when taking my cocker spaniel 'Lassie' for a walk up the
lane past his home. If he was in the garden he would come to
talk to me and discuss fishing amongst other matters and on one
such occasion he asked me whether I would like to accompany
him on an outing to Cefni Reservoir in Anglesey. It was a club
competition and I could have a lift there with him. Having
cleared it with my parents I accepted and plans were made for
the following Saturday afternoon, the competition would be
from 5pm to 9pm off the bank for the 'Welsh Salmon and Trout
Association Challenge Shield'.

My father acquired some lake flies for me from somewhere
during the week and I recall that for most of that Saturday I was
preparing and checking my tackle over, making casts
and the like and also watching the clock for I was to be ready by
3pm.

On the journey to Anglesey I was given a small envelope by Mr
Jones and it contained two flies a 'Mallard and Claret' and a
welsh pattern called 'Haul-a-Gwynt' (Sun and Wind), both on a
size 12 hook. (Page 196) A number of anglers that I had
previously met on the River Dwyfawr were present and they all
set off for various locations from the clubhouse some walking
over the dam wall and others going off over the railway line that
split the lake into two. I located myself in between two anglers

on the side of the railway line and fished away in the breeze, stopping to re-arrange the cast after a close encounter with a trout and a welcome cup of tea from a flask to wash down a sandwich my mother had prepared for me.

When I arrived back at the clubhouse for the weigh-in I was fishless, apart from that smash take to the 'Haul-a-Gwynt' I had been given. To see some of the trout on the scales whetted the appetite for more lake fishing experience - there being some great fish up to two pounds in weight - some silver like the Sea trout from the Dwyfawr and others with bulging golden bellies. During the course of the competition I had noticed an angler arriving at the water at about 8pm and fishing off the corner of the dam wall next to the club house, he was casting into the wind and, retrieving his flies figure of eight fashion, I saw him catch two fish on my approach to him as he fished on in the twilight.. He was a local angler and not involved with the competition, it was interesting to see him fish away in an unhurried fashion and he explained to me that the trout became more active towards the twilight which was in keeping with the way the Seatrout came into their own on the Dwyfawr at home, that was another one into the memory bank together with the flies he showed me, Mallard and Claret and a Butcher, size 12 and 14.

In many a subsequent conversation with Mr Jones he also parted some reliable information on lake fishing and of the pattern 'Haul-a-Gwynt' taken off my cast by that Cefni lake trout. I was able to get a supply of these from a hairdresser come fishing-tackle shop at Blaenau- Ffestiniog - I have a recollection of calling there with my father when he went to visit, in that town, a friend of his from his army days.

I went to the club competition again the following year for yet another blank session and decided that I needed to get some serious practice in at the lake game before pitting my skills against such accomplished anglers. My experiences from the River Dwyfawr and the River Wen in a flood were a far cry from the approach needed to tackle a Lake or Reservoir, fish behaviour, habitat, and feeding habits and the desired approach were totally different and new to me, one thing for certain the fish are always in charge and often surprise us, which takes me back to my first Salmon an experience several years before my introduction to Lake Trout. The fish came more by accident than skill I was yet again at the 'Widow's Pool' with my father in a roaring flood, this time on the inside bend of the river. My father had fished the fly in the rapidly clearing but high water all the way down the pool and I watched him change and reset the14ft greenheart with the worm cast ready for moving on. I pestered him repeatedly "Can I have a go?" Kindly as he was he put a worm on for me, instructing me to sit by a large boulder alongside the rough water entering the pool, whilst he took up the old tank aerial and spun a small spoon cast and step style 'Widow's Pool' was about fifty yards long of fishable water on the inside bend of the river.

An eel had taken most of the worm off the hook; I'd lifted it to the surface twice. Having watched my father overhead cast with the fly I decided that if I was to learn anything then I needed to have a go at the overhead cast. With worm tackle to the fore replicating what I had seen my father do, away I went, and I was astonished I could cast it a fair way onto the glide, maybe the lead weights had more to do with it than my skills. The delivery fashion was immaterial at the time the line landed fairly straight and after a couple of casts and allowing the business end to drift through the glide, I heard my father shouting at me to stop. I ignored the command and pretended not to have heard and would make use of the fact that I was unable to hear him due to the noise of the rough water at the head of the pool as by this time he was a good distance down the pool away from me and I also felt quite safe that I would not be collared for failing to do as I was told. I continued with my newly found skill and through the corner of my eye could see my father look back over his shoulder at me a couple of times but said nothing. My casting may have impressed him but there was no time even to consider that, for all of the sudden everything went tight and the rock which I thought I'd caught moved slowly out across the pool to the other side in the fast current. My heart was in my throat, I pulled hard and the business end pulled back harder with the greenheart bent over double. Panic, adrenaline rush, through to total elation at the occasion of that heavy rod bent almost double was another memory that will never leave me and to get my voice working also proved difficult but through it all I started shouting at the top of my voice, 'Salmon! Salmon!, Salmon!'. My father made his way up the pool slowly cursing away at me, accusing me of being stuck on a rock; I was almost in tears thinking I would get into serious trouble. He took hold of the rod and applied some side pressure to find that my statement was very accurate and after an immense battle the fish was brought to the side and landed, it was all of 9 lb (Page 24) and brand spanking new from the sea. Needless to say, I carried the fish myself all the way back to the road through some very rough terrain, there was no way I would allow my father to carry my fish although with out him I doubt whether the fish would have been banked. I'll never for get it the journey home was very quick on the Speed twin, I also carried it into the house and lifted it onto the drain board, another proud moment. My mother said it took a week for the smile on my face to wear off, how many times did I go up to that fish to examine it and take an estimate of its measurement in between my hands walking back into the lounge with my hands apart to show how big it really was and so I could tell my friends about it, well I was grown up now I was nine. (Page25) What a contrast there was fishing in a flood with a worm and on a falling water with a fly and the fact that the Salmon took the remnants of a worm roughly presented on the swing and through to the calmness and finesse required to tackle the Lake trout.

Unbeknown to me at that time of learning the various methods involved to secure a fish, a competitive element was growing in me daily in my quest to catch them and this no doubt developed over the years to follow in my father's footsteps in his achievements within the Club competition - of catching the heaviest Seatrout of the season from the River Dwyfawr at night. This won him the 'Coronation Cup' in 1958,1959, 1960, three years on the trot – some achievement by any standards. Plaques were awarded as keep sakes for each of the wins of the

'Coronation Cup' but rightfully in view of the three successive wins, the 'Cup' itself became his own. My father many years later informed me that through a verbal agreement with the Committee, he loaned it to the Association for continuance of the competition on the understanding that he could claim it if at any time he gave up fishing or was no longer a member of the Club, a mistake that he will never live down. He considered this at length and in his eightieth year whilst still a member he approached the Association Committee by way of a letter to register his wish for the Cup to adorn the sideboard at his home, with the offer of purchasing another 'Cup' for the Association for continuance of the competition. The Committee replied by letter that they had checked through their records for any note of the agreement reached in 1961, but unfortunately no written record could be found and for that reason decided not to grant my father his wish despite his offer to purchase another Cup. Needless to say he did not renew his membership.

His comfort is the knowledge that the 'Coronation Cup' is rightfully his despite the Committee's decision and that no one else in 50 years has achieved what he did.

I climbed onto the trophy ladder in 1970 when I again fished Cefni Reservoir in the Club competition and was narrowly beaten into second place by a few ounces. My two trout of 1lb 4oz and 1lb 6oz. qualified me to fish another competition for a place in the Welsh Salmon and Trout Association National Team and I ended up blanking off the bank at Trawsfynydd Lake some weeks later, more skills required!, back to the drawing board.

Bailiffing

The whole idea of poachers sickened my father and he had carried an honorary Bailiffs Warrant Card for a few years. When a vacancy came up for a full time water bailiff's position on the Rivers Llyfni, Gwyrfai and Seiont, driving the milk tanker to earn his keep became a memory as he secured the job and as a result another angle to the fishing world opened up within my life. Needless to say by this time in my life I needed no encouragement and a copy of the Salmon and Freshwater Fisheries Act 1963 was in pride of place in the paper rack alongside the fireplace and when my father was not reading it, I would delve into the pages and found the various statute laws intriguing, far more interesting than any of the books I had from school.

His new work was varied and included: the running of a small hatchery at Glangwna, Caernarfon; patrolling the rivers; checking on anglers licences and the stalking, apprehension and prosecution of poachers. Accompanying my father on these various exercises meant that I met many an angler who used various tactics within their chosen pastime. Some of them were especially good at it too and I picked up some exceptional tips. To put it into context, those were the days of plenty; the rivers were full to the brim with Salmon and Sea trout. It was also, however, the moment when problems began to set in, stocks were beginning to decline and the start of the demise of some of the fisheries in our time was becoming a reality. I recall Doctor William Jones from Liverpool University and his students on field visits carrying out surveys on the rivers and spawning streams I helped my father electro fishing where fish stocks and aquatic insects were monitored with detailed accounts of their presence or lack of. Each juvenile fish was measured and returned over a certain river section and then that very same stream would be examined twelve months on to establish growth rates and available food within.

Spawning time would come and go - netting the Salmon, stripping and fertilizing the ova and daily checking in the hatchery, removing the whitened eggs with a pipit. Eggs that were infertile within a tray containing hundreds would soon become white and a fungal growth would develop. Should the whitened eggs not be removed the fungal growth would extend to the fertile eggs and kill them off. Although a laborious task in almost freezing conditions it was a very necessary one. Ensuring that the right quantity and quality of water travelled through the eggs also had to be monitored. The next spring the small-unfed fry would be shared out to streams that carried enough aquatic food for their sustainability through the fry stage and into the Parr stage. That was the stage at which the fish would find their own way into the main rivers prior to maturing as smolts and start on that epic journey across the oceans to their sea feeding grounds. The turnover in nature of these wonderful fish always has and always will amaze me.

It was the returning fish that would be of great interest to the poachers, be they gangs operating nets and poisons or individuals using gaffs, spears, snares and the like to remove fish for personal gain. The dinner table at home would be full of stories about these events as they occurred and plans were hatched to apprehend the poachers at known locations.

It was on a warm Sunday morning in early June that I accompanied my father to the upper part of the River Llyfni just below Pen y Groes. He had told my mother that we would be back for our dinner by 1pm. On the way, he would stop at certain locations and look through his field glasses along the river in all directions. To do this, he would park and hide the mini van and walk to a vantage point. Sometimes he would turn round immediately and go back to the van and move location. Often he took his instructions from nature e.g. in wooded areas where the river could not be observed clearly, he would wait for a crow, a pigeon, or heron to fly along the river and also would watch the sheep and cattle in fields alongside the river – their behaviour was a sure fire give-away if there was some human presence.

At the old railway line the road went through a small tunnel and we left the van out of sight there walking down the road for a couple of hundred yards using the hedge alongside the road to shield our approach. Dad stopped a couple of times and looked through gaps onto the fields near the river and then continued to a farm gateway where I was told to sit on a staging created for the collection of milk churns. We had been there for possibly half an hour when he reached for his field glasses whispering to me, "We've got company, keep your head down". I had no idea what he had seen and he moved away from me giving me a hand signal to stay put.

I tried to look through the gap but could see nothing and the river was two short fields away with a number of bushes and large stones in the marshy field in front. My father returned and said to me that on the previous day he had walked the riverbank down and observed where foliage had been trampled near to some tree stumps on the opposite side of the river to us. This had made him suspicious that someone had been looking into the river at that point. He also said that further down at another location half a field away he had collected a fresh Salmon scale off a stone alongside another trampled area in and amongst some trees. Certainly not an area fishable off that particular bank, but a location where Salmon lied up under tree roots and alongside large boulders.

The wooded bank and field on the opposite side of the river rose sharply through bracken and gorse onto a very large open field in the general direction of Pen-y-Groes village and he pointed out to me, through the gap, two men sitting right on top of the bank facing us, surveying the area. He explained that we would have to move quickly and quietly if the two men came down towards the river where they would be hidden from view by the riverside foliage and trees, in order that we could get to a better vantage point near to the river to observe further.

No sooner than he had said this, the men got to their feet and walked down the bank in the direction of the river. Dad and I were up the farm lane, through a gate and alongside a blackthorn hedge that run down towards the river in a few seconds. By this time my heart was pumping vigorously, wondering what would happen.

We stopped and from our crouched position behind the hedge observed further. My father turned to me and said that he could see one of the men still on the bank some distance above the river and that if and when he moved towards the river we could cross the small field to another location where we could have cover of some low bushes and a few large boulders to screen us from view. We would have to move quickly and quietly through the rushes and if he stopped I was to do the same and lie flat on the field.

He kept scanning around with the field glasses and all of the sudden he said "right, now", and off he went with me close behind. We were able to reach the desired vantage point and by this time I could hear the noise of the water rushing between the stones and when I moved my head I could see the water tumbling and glistening in the sunlight through the branches of the riverside bushes. I was warned to keep my head down and he again pointed to a large stone some thirty or so yards away in the open field in front, which would be the next stopping point, no more than 15 yards from the river. I took another peep around the corner of the bush and could just about make out, through the trees, the men on the riverbank further upstream. One of them had his hands raised and roofed above his eyes looking into the river, shielding his eyes from the sun. They then moved upstream away from us and at that point my father gave me the sign to move and off we went again.

The sheltering stone was not as large as it had seemed and we were both on our hands and knees close up behind it, and to each other. No need to describe further than to say my nose was positioned in a rather un-desirable location. however my excitement was such that that did not occur to me in spite of small panicky farts all round. My father turned around and whispered to me, that they would get nothing upstream where they were looking but that there was a good lie for salmon under the far bank almost opposite our position. He also told me that if they got a fish we would rush them and apprehend them. Then he resumed his original position so he could see around the edge of the stone through a small clump of rushes and gave me a thumbs up sign. I took a peep over the stone to see that the men were now right above the position my father had pointed out to me.

In the excitement that followed he again let off this time substantially as he set himself in position for the off and I had no choice but to live with it as I was too frightened to move. Holding my breath was my salvation. Then I heard a splashing noise from the river, followed by voices and within seconds my father gave the sign to move. This was a huge relief, I was glad as I could breathe again. He was up to his feet and running at the river shouting something like 'Water Bailiff' on the top of his voice, and at running speed and never breaking his stride he jumped right into the middle of the river towards the poachers landing with an almighty splash and, on impact, almost disappearing into the deep pool a few feet away from the two men. The river Llyfni is about 15ft wide at that point. As you can imagine, there was a major panic on the far bank, as the two poachers struggled to make their getaway. I can just picture it today they ran into one another and tripped over the gorse and bracken in their haste and indeed quite possibly terror at this wild man leaping into the river in front of them.

My father charged out of the river onto the other bank and shouted for me to cross the river and follow them so that he could get the fish. I was able to jump from stone to stone and get across the river without getting wet, but by this time both poachers were clean away and half way up the field. I kept with them, following up the bank, across the field and onto the railway line. There I picked up a path and followed them at a distance into a wooded area near to a housing estate, where I lost sight of them. I doubt it if they had been aware of my presence and I was able to locate them as I could hear one of them being sick.

I positioned myself within earshot of them and waited for my father who soon caught up with me. He handed me a Salmon and a sharp three-pronged garden fork with a long handle to it. (Page 28)The poor fish had been speared and almost cut in half in the process - the poachers already had the fish on the bank, killing it as we approached them. Thus although we could not save the fish, the actions of my father in jumping into the river the way he did had resulted in the poachers dropping the Salmon and pronged spear. My father insisted, on the 'element of surprise' being a handy tool in the circumstances. He told me to stay put with the Salmon and spear and went into the wood after them. I watched from a distance as he talked with one of the poachers, who, whilst still throwing up, he protested his innocence stating that he'd just been walking along the riverbank when he saw someone take a fish out. I don't think they hurried back to the river after that experience.

Sunday dinner was a triumphant if rather belated affair and the story of the morning was proudly related to my mother. My farther returned to Penygroes that afternoon and called at the local Police Station where an Officer gave assistance in the identity of the second culprit. Both poachers eventually appeared in the local Magistrates court and were heavily fined.

That was the first of many an encounter of poachers that I experienced - 'Bailiffing' in the company of my father. I also learnt other things from him on those bailffing visits - in low water he would take me to locations and show me tails sticking out from under roots of trees, which if you did not know about them, you would never have noticed. He knew every lie and almost the entire stock of Salmon and Sea trout running these rivers. This in-depth knowledge was an integral and necessary part to successful bailiffing – a useful lesson for me in my later career, applying as it does to more than just bailiffing .

My father often worked alongside another bailiff Bill Bayliss, from Caernarfon, who owned a pack of hounds and was a regular huntsman in his spare time. The hounds were kept in an old building in Llanrug and they were operated as a foot pack, with guns. Another wonderful memory from the 'bailiffing days'. Indeed the baying of the hounds in full cry became a favourite sound, far better in truth than the electric guitar I had at home when I briefly had aspirations of following in Elvis Presley's footsteps. (Page 28).

Moving on in life and mapping my future

At the age of 16 I became the proud owner of a Bantam Major Motor Cycle 125 cc - it was a number of years old and the horn was a black rubber ball type set behind the front lamp It went 'Beep' 'Beep' as you squeezed. It was my pride and joy. I recall my mother and I setting about hand painting the machine in a green coloured paint. The bike was important to me and fishing took back stage for a while when I also discovered 'girls', played the guitar and formed a band, much to my father's disgust. However I did not totally abandon my obsession for fishing and still went quite often, but sort of became a little more independent of it and about things in general I suppose as is the way with most boys when they become young men.

I left school with just a scraping of GCE qualifications and went to work at T.J.Williams 'Wool Merchants' at Porthmadog. I was employed in the Shop and Office selling animal health drugs and other related products to farmers.

I was trained to repair shearing machine handsets and did quite a bit of this for the farmers that came in. I had in fact never been shearing myself and accepted an invite to Cwm Prysor Farm, near Trawsfynydd, to try my hand at it. This was a hill farm and it had three mountain lakes thereon so I was reminded to bring my fishing rod with me and that we would have a cast after the shearing had been completed. Needless to say I needed no encouragement.

I recall that the shearing was not an easy task and also caused severe back pain. We were in a corrugated tin shed in searing heat and I can remember sweat pouring off me as I tackled the shearing having first watched two or three of the animals being snipped. The shed we were in had only a small doorway to it and it was relatively dark inside. All of a sudden it went darker when in the doorway stood a large woman, the farmers mother, holding a stainless steel bucket. Everyone stopped as she dipped cups into the bucket and handed them out, I first thought that it was milk as it was white, but in fact it was half milk and half water. It certainly helped quench the thirst and was most welcome.

When the shearing was over I was invited into the house for tea and told to wash my hands in the dairy outside. Inside the dairy there was a wooden barrel with a handle on it stood on a stand. I was later to learn that this was used to make butter and at that moment when I looked out through a side window I could see the old lady I had seen earlier out in the field with a cow tied to a post and there she was milking away by hand into the stainless steel bucket, I'd heard of this but never seen it before there were modern milking machines, but time had stood still at 'Cwm Prysor'.

Tea was a slice of home cured ham which was very salty followed by a generous helping of boiled new potatoes mixed with butter milk (the milk left over after the butter had been made) called in welsh (tatws llaeth). I also recall the old lady returning to the house and cutting the bread just like I had seen my grandmother do it, throwing the slices off the knife onto a plate in a central position on the table. The slices were like wafers and she buttered and sliced as we ate away. Her piny was made out of sacking material that went all the way round her and reached right down to the floor, similar in size to those big wool sacks I had filled with the sheared fleeces earlier, that butter was something else, quite salty but it was delicious.

Away we went and fished Treweryn Lake right on the top of the hill above the farm before making our way to another smaller lake on another hill some distance away Llyn Cors Barcud (The Lake of the Kite's Gorse or Moor). We eventually arrived back at the farm yard just as the light failed for the day and we had a great bag of trout in the 6 to 8 oz bracket, beautifully marked and coloured, that was shared equally between us. A real wild trout day and nothing has ever tasted as fine as those beautiful fresh, white-fleshed brown trout.

I recall several further visits to Llyn Cors Barcud and one day I managed to catch a three pound trout from it and although it had the typical large head of a cannibal, to me it was a beauty of wondrous proportions and put up a great account of itself on the size 16 Coch-y-Bonddu fly.

I decided to close down my motor cycling days when three close friends lost their young lives on them in quick successsion and I swapped it for a Mini Van. My father had purchased a brand new MG1100 in two-tone green and cream, it was that car I passed my driving test in at the first attempt. Once I got some proper wheels however, the guitar and my attempt at a pop group were soon abandoned as I went on to other things in my life.

After about a year I was bored to tears with my lot in work but I had to keep working to pay my way. Suddenly there appeared out of the blue, a golden opportunity, the Gwynedd River Division had a vacancy for a trainee water bailiff working on the River Conway. I believe that it was part of a fund-aided set up and it would necessitate moving from home and living in that area, My father was able to secure an interview for me with the Fisheries Superintendent, the late Herbert Evans and the Head Bailiff, the late Emrys Lloyd Price, both very experienced in fisheries. Both persons were totally dedicated to the cause as evidenced by a vicious incident involving poachers on the River Dovey some years previous in which Emrys Price had lost an eye and Herbert Evans a spell in hospital with several broken bones. I think that night one of the poachers had lost his life - when he was trying to avoid capture, running away in the darkness, he fell into the river and drowned, so I was aware of the risks involved.

My father's loyalty and dedication to the cause and possibly the fact that I had assisted him on many an encounter swayed in my favour and I secured the post. Shortly after that I left home for the first time in my life to move into lodgings with May and Violet Williams at Bryn Llwyd, Nebo Road in Llanrwst, a real home from home - they certainly took care of me.

During the course of the next eighteen months I gained experience in all aspects of 'Bailiffing'. In the main I would work alongside Emrys Price on the Conway, but also worked with other bailiffs in North Wales on many a surveillance exercise against poaching. As it was at the very end of the Salmon season that I joined the Gwynedd River Division, my first efforts were mainly directed at Cae Du Hatchery and, that winter, we managed to fill it to capacity with Ova from various rivers. We looked after them during the winter and planted them out in the small rivers and lakes at the top end of the river systems the following spring as unfed fry, very many thousands of them, laborious work, carrying out heavy plasticised bags containing water and thousands of fish, sometimes up to a mile away from where the vehicle was parked.

I recall that winter visiting Alaw reservoir in Anglesey and joining the bailiffs there having made hundreds of yards of Fyke nets at Cae Du Hatchery under the supervision and to the exacting standards of Herbert Evans. We'd set them in the deep ditches for trapping trout and one day I recall being stood in the front end of a rubber dingy travelling slowly up the lake to check the nets, having to break the ice with an oar on the way. Those wild trout in Alaw in 1968 were something else, up to six and seven pound in weight.

The spring came and I met the commercial netsmen on the lower Conway, fishing for a fish called 'Brwyniad' in Welsh I think it was some kind of 'Smelt' but cannot be certain of that, your hands smelt of cucumber when you had handled one. Another main priority them days was to shoot as many 'Cormorants' as we could to protect the stock of Salmon 'Smolts' on their sea migration run. I was used to shooting, as that was the pastime during the winter months when the Salmon and Sea trout were in the closed season. I also recall going with the Head Bailiff to the harbour at Porthmadog and netting the 'Mullet' there and selling them around the restaurants in Rhyl and Prestatyn, the money being used to buy the cartridges to tackle the cormorant problem. It was the 'sensible' thing to do and we just got on with it, unhampered by all the types of restrictions in evidence today.

The spring and summer of 1968 brought with it a major run of Salmon and Sea trout into the Conway, together with problems of poaching in all its guises. There was also a major pollution incident on the River Ogwen and I spent days there collecting dead Salmon, Sea trout, Trout and Eels, from 1year old Parr through to adult fish returning to spawn - a sight that saddened me in the extreme. (Page 29).

I recall coming from Conway one night with the Head Bailiff having been to check the Estuary. Near to a row of houses between Trefriw and Dolgarrog, we noticed a car with a roof rack thereon parked in a lay-by. The car was unknown to us, it was after midnight and all the lights were out in the houses. I was sent to check the tax disc on the screen and came back to report, 'Post Office, Conway'. The Head Bailiff was suspicious and decided to call in Trefriw Police Station where after a short discussion the local Constable accompanied us back to where the car was parked. We hid the van we were in and proceeded onto the river bank across a field from the road. I was left in the reeds near to the river with a radio and the Head Bailiff and the Officer went back to watch the car in the Lay By. As I was used to the sounds of the night I easily picked out the noise of oars being used and reported this very quietly on the two way radio to the Head Bailiff. I held station and heard splashing noises of fish being taken out of a net, I'd heard a similar noise some years earlier in a harbour with my father in the dead of night. I reported this too.

After about an hour I could hear, not too far away upstream of me, a hissing noise which I could not decipher and a trampling noise in the reeds at the edge of the river followed shortly afterwards by two figures walking on the embankment above me, carrying something between them on their shoulders. I could make them out against the skyline, I waited for them to go a reasonable distance before reporting this to the Head Bailiff and followed up the embankment and along the path from the river towards the road. When I was about 25 yards from the road I heard a thud and squeaking of the field gate opposite to where I had seen the car parked in the lay-by, torches came on and there was shouting. In the torchlight I could see one person running back towards me so I ducked in the long grass and as he went past stuck my foot out which brought him to ground and winded him. I placed my knee in his back just to hold him down and within seconds the Head Bailiff was with me and we led him back to the road where he was put into the custody of the Police Officer. The other poacher had made good his escape. On the roadside near to the gate I examined and unpacked a rubber dingy wrapped and tied around two oars, there was a gill net and thirteen Salmon and Sea trout contained within. The dingy explained the hissing noise that I could not decipher earlier, the air being released from it. We never traced the poacher that escaped but the one we had caught received a hefty fine at Conway Magistrates Court.

I worked a five and a half day week and sometimes I would go off home for my day off and other times I would stay and walk to a mountain lake to fish. I would take myself away from the main rivers as I was on them every day and I honed my lake fishing skills at Llyn Elsi and other small mountain lakes around Betws y Coed. I fished wet flies in a team of three on a cast, my favourites being a Connemara Black on the point sometimes changing that with a Dunkeld, a 'Coch y Bonddu' on the middle dropper and my favourite Haul a Gwynt on the top dropper position. I began to realise that the more I fished the lakes the more I liked that style of fishing and of course the scenery and the sense of being at one with nature all helped with that growing affection for lake fishing, especially so mountain lakes that were not easily accessible.

Late in that summer of 1968 the dreaded Salmon disease, Ulcerative Dermal Necrosis (UDN) made an appearance – the poor fish were covered in a white fungus and dying by the dozen. I had never seen the like of it before and I sincerely hope that I never have to encounter it again, it seemed to attack some fish as soon as they entered the river system and for some reason other fish survived spawning through to the colder months and then became infected. We were careful again to collect eggs from fish that showed no signs of disease, and in order to try to alleviate the problem of fish rubbing up against one another and transferring the disease we removed the dead and very diseased ones from the river on a daily basis. Some were buried in lime and others carted away in the mini van I used for work, crammed with bags of dead Salmon and Sea trout and taken to the incinerator at Penmaenmawr. Very many hundreds of them were despatched in this way over a period of time, and that was from the Conway and its tributaries alone. The effect of this disease for the nation as a whole was devastating and must have contributed to the demise of the Salmon as we see it today.

Whilst I was at Llanrwst a friend of my father's from his army days, Taliesyn Edwards, a Police Inspector for the area was stationed at Abergele. He was also an angler and I used to call at his home to see him and share a cup of tea if I was in that area. We used to talk of the various characters I came across in the course of my work and it was then that I started to realise that my fishing adventures were becoming less and less and my job taking more and more of my time. I don't think that I went to fish the Dwyfawr that summer at all and that in itself was totally alien to my nature compared to the preceding years.

I recall Taliesyn Edwards telling me that I should join the Police Force as the conditions of service were far superior to that of a 'Water Bailiff' with working hours, holidays and a good pension scheme, I let this pass me for a while but it lurked at the back of my mind and came to a head when, one Thursday, I called at Betws-y-Coed Police Station, to find out what time I was due in Court the following Tuesday with a poaching case. The Officer I spoke to could not tell me and when I said I would call to see him on the Friday, he told me he was off Friday, Saturday,

Sunday, Monday, but he would leave a note for me. I pricked up my ears at this and asked him whether he was on holiday and he explained that once every month because of the way rest days were structured he would have a long weekend off. That did it, it was too much for me to ignore and I made the necessary moves and filled in the application. I recall the Interview with the Chief Constable who looked over his glasses at me stood to attention in front of him as I had been directed to, "Why does a Police Officer carry a staff?" (Truncheon) he asked, I was lost but knew I had to say something, "To defend himself if he is viciously attacked, Sir", cough, splutter, 'No son, to enforce the law when all other methods have failed, you're a bit short but I'll give you a chance", "Thank you Sir". Some change in attitudes over the years, aye!

I worked a fortnight's notice and then had a two-week holiday break, before going away for three months training. The mini van was traded in for a Wolseley Hornet and off I went to Manchester to see my father's friend Jim Sullivan, mentioned earlier. Now Jim Sullivan was in the demolition and sand and gravel business, he was on site one day and picked up a brick and threw it up to the back of the wagon. When he bent over to pick up another brick off the floor disaster struck when the brick he had thrown up onto the load, fell back off the wagon and struck him a sharp blow on his spine. He never walked again, was wheelchair bound and his fishing days were over. In spite of this he was wonderful company and I had a great time taking him all over the Manchester area in the Wolsley, he wanted to visit several sites where his sons were working, it was when the M62 and M60 were being built, and he was supplying sand and gravel to various large companies. Jim Sullivan, not a racist by any means of the imagination, chuckled to himself , a through and through Irishman selling part of England back to the English.

My training at Bridgend for three months was soon over and I was posted to Wrexham to work the town. I found lodgings, sharing with another Officer, Paul Dodd, who was also an angler, needless to say we struck it off instantly and we had something in common outside the policing routine to discuss. I'll never forget that first day walking down the main street - I thought that everyone was looking at me. Some were polite but from others came sideways glances of hate. Anyway I soon realised that it was the uniform that drew the glances of hate and I settled in.

Paul Dodd took me to Llangollen and we fished the River Dee out of someone's garden. It was then that I encountered my first Grayling, a beauty of about a pound, taken on a worm. Paul was intrigued with my style of presentation honed over the years, and he showed me his style with a float.

I took little interest in the Dee with the Salmon and the Sea trout in those days as I used to spend my days off with my parents and my enthusiasm for the local Dwyfawr, Wen, Erch was re-kindled. Although the stocks had been decimated with the UDN disease, there were still fish coming in and the disease continued to affect them in the rivers in the winter when the cold weather set in. On reflection the winters were much colder then than they are now but on some of the summer floods I took great bags of fish from the upper Dwyfor, Sea trout to six pounds and Salmon to fourteen pounds. (Page 98).

One thing that struck home to me was that the Brown Trout and the Eel stocks were declining at an alarming rate; the same was noticed in the Wen and the Erch where I still fished when the conditions were right. Something was definitely wrong and as my father was still working as a Water Bailiff we discussed the issue at great length. In his opinion there was a lack of food in the rivers, fly hatches were also in decline and he broached the subject of liming the land mentioning that that the subsidy to the farmers had been halted by the ministry and that land drainage had become obsessive. This meant that the rivers would rise quickly after rain and would drop to normal level nearly as quickly afterwards, there being no sponge left in the land and since the sieving effect of the bogs was no longer present, all impurities washed into the rivers quickly. He felt it was something to do with the upsetting of that balance plus the effect of what we describe today as 'Acid Rain'.

We were discussing these things as far back as the early 70's and here we are in 2009, thirty odd years down the line still talking about it. I have serious thoughts about the lack of direction from successive governments and the inactivity of the Ministry then and of DEFRA now in not applying common sense to the issue. Since lime is an 'Alkaline' which will counteract 'Acidity' to a certain degree, why not reverse the decision to pay grants to the farmers to lime the land? A little is better than nothing and certain fishing clubs have enhanced their fisheries through carrying lime to their small lakes and raising the PH factor of the water encouraging aquatic insects and increasing the numbers and growth in the resident trout. I just cannot comprehend the fact that this still falls on deaf ears - it is quite simple and would have more of a positive than a negative effect, a little is better than nothing.

Strange Characters & Chasing that elusive Cap

I was on night duty on foot patrol in Wrexham Town Centre in the days when Wrexham was a mining area and there also existed the Wrexham Larger works. To say that the main problems were drunken miners is an understatement, burglary and thieving was rife by comparison to the quiet village I had hailed from. It was all heavy on me to start with to see the effects of crime and the resulting pain, sadness and suffering for its victims. I don't believe that I ever became hardened to it but got used to the bustle of town life although quietly I longed for that old village life and its serenity.

I cannot remember what day of the week it was but I was set to go in to the station for my break at 2am. The other foot patrol officer and mobile support for the town were in at 1am, so I was the only one out in the town centre, between one and two.

I had bid goodnight to a couple of stragglers and of course in them days we used to handshake all the shop doors front and back. It was my responsibility to look after my beat and I was very aware from the pre shift briefing that over some weeks there had been a number of burglaries in shops by smashing the plate glass windows and stealing from within.

Just after 1am I had walked from the town centre through Hope Street, Queen Street, Rhosddu Road to the top end of King Street opposite the War Memorial Hospital. You would not recognise the place today as it was then - it's all changed apart from the position of the streets. I was extremely hungry and I dug into my pocket and found a sixpenny piece. I made my way back to

Queen Street, where I knew there was a Chocolate Box Shop, which carried a Nestle machine on the wall outside. The shop doorway was set back in off the street as were most of the shops. I got a bar of chocolate and as I stood for five minutes or so in the doorway devouring it and enjoying every bite, there was an almighty crash and tingling of breaking glass. Off Queen Street ran Lampbitt Street, Henblas Street, Hope Street and Rhosddu Road but I had no idea from which street the noise had come from. However my training over the years with Bailiffing practices had taught me to stop and think and respond, not to react. I knew the burglar was there and he had no knowledge of my presence, so the 'element of surprise' factor went through my mind from my escapades with my father on the river Llyfni. The darkest of the Streets was Henblas Street about fifty yards away from where I was stood on the opposite side of the road, I lifted my cloak back over my shoulders, removed my helmet and tip toed across the road, those 'Air Wear' boots were a godsend, quiet and light.

I continued to make my way to the corner of Queen Street and Henblas Street and went into the doorway of Wrights Corner Shop, a ladies clothing store. I stood motionless in the shadow from what little light there was and listened. to a strange noise from very close by. Now by this time the adrenalin was rushing round my body and my heart was thumping away. The windows in the shop were set back in both Queen Street and Henblas Street and substantial brick pillars separated them. I crept quietly to the edge of the pillar leading down Henblas Street and peeped round. I could see nothing in the distance down the street and thought to myself that I'd made a mistake on the location of the noise. I held position and to my amazement from the other side of the very pillar I was stood against in Henblas Street, I saw within a yard of me in the available light shining from Hope Street someone in a semi crouched position. I looked down and could just make out the sparkle of the broken glass on the street, then the rustle of feet on the same glass. I put my helmet down and quietly and cautiously stepped out to watch him pull a long garment out from the shop through the Venetian blinds and proceed to wrap it up. I leapt on his back and at the same time shouted "Police you are under arrest!"

Well, he stood up straight and dropped the garment, I had him in a headlock, my feet left the floor as he tried to free himself, by turning round vigorously shaking from side to side. He was huge in all ways and his hand went completely around my forearm. We struggled into the light in Queen Street, and as he turned his head round, I looked into his face noticed he had a crew cut hairstyle and that one eye looked straight at me whilst the other looked directly at his broken nose! At that moment, he lost his balance in the struggle and fell to his knees but I was able to maintain mine and he said, "He's gone off down there" pointing down Henblas Street. I still maintained my hold on him and replied "Good you're my main witness then". To my amazement this huge man then started to cry and I raised the alarm for assistance with my pocket radio. I could hear the tyres on the Police vehicle screeching out of the Police Station Yard and within seconds he had been bundled into the van and we were on the way back to the Station. On arrival the duty Sergeant Daryl Jones after hearing the facts sent me to the canteen, next door to the charge room for a cup of tea whilst other officers assisted to take him into the cell corridor.

The Sergeant then came to the canteen and praised me for my actions. I was a bit shaky but managed not to spill the tea, when from the cell corridor came bursts of laughter. The duty officer came into the canteen and was laughing uncontrollably, pointing in the direction of the cell passage. Another officer went to take a look and came back for me. There, stood outside the cell door, was my prisoner in, you will never guess, a bra and panties. Although amused I stood there in disbelief because as well as the ladies undergarments he'd had such a fright on his arrest that he had messed himself. It was the most bizarre sight and very different from what I had imagined was my foe when I first grabbed him.

A Detective was called out and he took over the case. If memory serves me right I think he cleared about seven of the town centre burglaries with one stroke and they all involved ladies clothing mainly under garments. That night our cross-dressing friend had taken a light blue coloured dressing gown, which would never have fitted or suited him. Such stupidity I thought, and in my own rather countrified way, it also disgusted me somewhat. At that young age I just could not get my mind focused on why he had chosen this path in his life, but I suppose it takes all kinds. My fetish was fishing and you bet I am glad of that, just imagine…no it doesn't bear a thought, we'll leave it there!

Very many years later, when my daughter was eighteen, she had gone to one of the nightclubs in Wrexham and we had made arrangements for me to pick her up at 1am. I had warned her not to wait outside for me and that I would knock on the door when I arrived. When I did so, the door flew open and there stood holding the door, in full doorman regalia, bow tie and all, was the very man I had last seen in his ladies undies – now hopefully buying them rather than stealing them – maybe not – perhaps it was the thrill of the whole business – stealing and cross-dressing that gave him his kicks. As I drove away with my daughter I wondered what under wear he might have had on tonight, somehow doubting that they would be a good pair of Y fronts!

During the free afternoons when on night shift, I would get down to the River Dee and spend a couple of hours on its banks. It was my escape from the intensity of the town lifestyle, and the strange characters I became involved with in one way or another. I am eternally grateful for my introduction to Angling, a release valve for that unsolicited stress and also a real leveller in reality, the fish are always in charge, you believe it, but that is another kind of stress.

Glancing through the 'General Orders' in work I saw a Country Station vacancy in Anglesey and I thought that perhaps my escape route out of Wrexham had arrived. I applied and indeed secured the post. More to the point, I now had Llyn Coron, Llyn Cefni, Llyn Alaw and the Dwyfawr only an hour away. It was 1971 when I returned to Llyn Cefni for a competition and I came in with a bag of five fish all taken on a small dry Coachman size 16, in bright sunshine. I had all the fish before 7pm, fishing the shallow area at the top end of the small lake. Wading out in and amongst the weed, my new plasticised floating level line was a dream compared to the silk line. Indeed I won the competition and again qualified to fish the final qualifying match for the International Welsh Team - this time on 'Claerwen' reservoir in mid Wales. Again alas I failed miserably in the final. That well known angler, journalist and secretary of the 'Welsh Salmon and Trout Angling Association' Moc Morgan OBE, who was a headmaster at that time won that match having walked over the hill to one of the bays. 'Brwynog Bay' it was called and he had a very impressive bag of trout from it. I recall him checking their measurement prior to weighing them in, on the bonnet of a car and I wondered at that time if it was his own car. Another recollection that day was seeing for the first time the Coch-y-Bonddu Beetle in droves along one shore. In a small ravine I picked up a bundle of them tied together in a ball shape, as big as a cricket ball. Wish I'd had a camera with me. At the Angling Club Annual Dinner I was presented with another Silver Cup WFFA Challenge Shield 1971 Winner, for my efforts on Llyn Cefni.

Whilst stationed in Anglesey I met up with a great character and a truly superb Lake fisher, John Ifor Thomas - a thinking angler and meticulous in preparation. We became close fish ing friends and spent many hours at Llyn Coron, Cefni and Alaw which John knew intimately. I picked up such a vast amount of information from John, on tackle, flies, techniques and approach that it enhanced my fishing immensely in a short space of time.

My work as a country policeman fitted in well with the need for spare time to go fishing. I had no fixed hours but was constantly on call, I would steal an hour here and there, but could do it at the right time to fish for the Brown Trout in the best taking times. I also had a family with two small children to care for and that did reduce the time available but the responsibility was mine. The work involved in my new job was totally different to working in a town because I soon realised that when you had to enforce the law on someone in a rural area, you only realised after some time that you'd upset the entire family who mostly lived in the same area and that created an atmosphere which again I was not accustomed to. Trying to get my mind round this policing game was not an easy task, for I could only see black or white if you get my drift. I never delved into the grey area, my upbringing had set my mind to knowing right and knowing wrong, there was nowhere in between. Perhaps this made me a better copper – who knows? I have an outside general view of what the grey area is but have no idea how to deal with it, neither did I or have I a wish to go there.

Fly fishing the competitive side

North Wales Police had a sports section, as did other forces throughout the United Kingdom who were affiliated to the Police Athletic Association. The fly-fishing section in North Wales was organised and ably run by another great angler Oscar Evans of Caernarfon. As time progressed I became Secretary of the fishing section and established contacts throughout the Police forces up and down England, Scotland, Wales and Northern Ireland, which started as a result of some Officers from North Wales visiting Edinburgh and meeting up at a Rugby match with a Lothian and Borders Police Sergeant, Dave Scougall, another great angler. He in turn invited North Wales Police to form a team and travel to fish Loch Leven in a match against the Scottish Police.

That was back in 1979, so it was down to Davy Scougall for kicking it all off. As a result of this chance meeting the match took place and arrangements were made for all Forces throughout England and Wales to be contacted to see if their sports organisations did in fact have a fishing section. Eventually after a positive response a meeting was convened and an organising committee set up. I became Secretary of the newly formed organisation and Brian Williams of the Gwent Police, Chairman - I believe that he still holds the position of Vice Chairman even though he retired a few years back. Chief Inspector Arthur Donaldson of the Strathclyde Force in Scotland a keen angler was involved, he was also on the committee of the Police Athletic Association Council and he encouraged and assisted our Committee to apply for 'Fly fishing' to be recognised as a 'Police Athletic Association Sport'. I recall drafting and posting the letter which met with the desired approval and as the Sports sections of the Police Athletic

Association was split into seven regions we had to arrange Regional matches from which teams were selected for an International Match and also a National Championship. This led to visits to Chew Valley Lake, Rutland Water, Grafham Water, Kielder Water, Llyn Brenig, Llandegfedd Reservoir, Loch Leven and Lake of Menteith in rotation, as the years rolled on. The troubles in Northern Ireland made it difficult to arrange a match there, but I do recall one being run and that they looked after us very well but it was for me, 'strange' to say the least with Police Officers carrying machine guns guarding us, dotted about all around the Lakes that were used. The competitions are still going and 2006 saw the 25th official Police International Match at Llyn Brenig.

My fishing time was totally taken up on the competitive side now and momentum was gaining towards securing that place on the full International Welsh Team. It was through Mike Green that I eventually had another stab at it. I received a phone call one evening to ask if I could represent the Federation of Brenig Anglers in a match at Llyn Brenig the following day, in a team of four. I hadn't been chosen for the team and got in as a last minute reserve. I happened to be off work and took up on the challenge, it was a bank match and we could go anywhere to fish. There was a great turnout and only after arriving at Brenig did I realise that it was a Welsh Salmon and Trout bank fishing Championship Team event and there were over a hundred anglers there from all over Wales. The other Federation team members were Mike Green, Dai Owen and Mike Plack. (Page 98).

I fished hard all day with little success although I did manage two stockie rainbows and a brown trout of about a pound in weight. Moving quite a number of times trying to locate fish was difficult because of the number of anglers present in the match. Late in the afternoon with an hour left, I got in a corner of a bay where the wind was blowing into and was able to cast across the wave at an angle but along the bank in a deep gully. I took eight further fish in quick succession on a fly that John Ifor Thomas had given me, a multicoloured tinsel body, more on that later. I arrived at the weigh in to find that there were several decent bags taken and the other lads in the team had also had some success albeit nowhere near what I had caught. Anxious moments after everyone had weighed in until the announcement that our team had won the Shield followed by a lot of backslapping and congratulations. It was a great feeling and then came the shock of finding out that I had secured a place in the final team selection and was invited to fish a boat competition at Llyn Trawsfynydd in a fortnight's time. My catch of eleven fish put me in the top forty from the Brenig match and we were to compete against each other to select a team of fourteen to represent Wales in the Autumn International Match the following year at Loch Harray in Orkney. I was drawn to fish with Ken Bowring from Cardiff, an established Welsh International and I agreed to arrange a boatman for the event. As soon as I got home I phoned my father and told him of the achievement and he agreed to look after the boat for us in the match. I was delighted with his support.

Preparation went on in earnest for a fortnight - tying casts, flies and making all kinds of enquiries about the Lake, methods, flies and the like - more intensely than I had ever prepared before. Competition day arrived and since I was surrounded by current, past and budding Internationals I did not hold out much hope. I had information about Tyn Twll Bay, Bailey Bridge, Main Dam and the Sticks area just off the Power Station. Anyway, off we went at ten o clock and there was to be eight hours serious fishing in front of us both. Ken was very pleasant company and talked about previous International matches and the fishing he did at Llandegfedd Reservoir. By lunchtime Ken had two fish in areas that I had not had any information about, but I persisted doggedly and my first fish came at about teatime to that same fly, the 'John Ifor Fly' as it became known.

We drifted into Tyn Twll bay but there were a number of boats in the area where I wanted to go, near to a sunken wall, then all of the sudden the wind died down completely into a flat calm and most of the boats went off in search of wind. As we passed boats and they passed us on the drift, hand signals showing one finger up and a wave back and to on the horizontal indicating a blank, was about the norm. My father pulled the boat up along side the wall on the oars and we fished away with only an hour left. A fish broke the surface to my left and I covered it with no response. It moved again a few yards away and again the same result. It was then that, I remembered about a little fly I had dressed and named 'Y Felan Fach' (the little yellow one, page 198) and quickly changed to it whilst my father held the boat on station. The fish moved again and Ken covered it as I had my line in the boat, again to no avail. Finally I cast the line out and fished away keeping an eye out in the area of the sunken wall. In the very light breeze in the sunlight I thought I saw the flash of a fish's flank and the slightest water surface disturbance. I covered the area and was into my second fish, which took the newly changed fly. It was promptly boated.

Ken's fish were heavier than mine and as we motored back for the weigh in, knowing that the top forty anglers from the previous match were out, I held little hope of qualifying with two fish, Ken calmly said, "You may well get in, I hope to with two, it's not a good fishing day". There were indeed many disappointed faces on the shore as we arrived. After what appeared to be a long wait the results were announced and 'yes!' I was in the Welsh team, my burning ambition fulfilled at last. It was an incredible feeling and the phone line was hot that evening as you can imagine because I wanted to tell the whole world.

When the realisation that I was a 'Welsh International' sank in properly and I'd come off that roller coaster feeling, the next thought in my mind was that I had to do really well and I knew that I could not leave that to chance.

Now that I had gained my cap, preparation began in earnest. I splashed out some savings, I bought myself a new Hardy Fred Buller five weight 'Drifter' eleven foot three inches long, a Hardy Perfect Reel and an ice blue floating line to match. The spare spool carried a Masterline Neutral density line knowing that it would suit the style of fishing that I did from a boat. It would be pertinent to make the point that Brown Trout were free risers and the stocked rainbows were also far more aggressive and would come to the surface far more readily than they do today. Whilst the wild brown trout still remain so, the stocked fish of today would appear to have that aggressiveness bred out of them. It may be something to do with the triploids that are stocked, I'm not sure, but I know that they are not the same as they used to be. It may also be a contributory factor that the fly hatches are not the same any more and stock fish tend to stay deep or at varying depths dependant on the depth of the daphnia that they gorge themselves on. In those days most of the boat fishing was done drifting broadside on and in the upper layers of water in front of the drifting boat, that is what I practiced. Tactics and approach were changing in certain areas though; e.g. rudder fishing with lead core lines was prevalent in the Midlands Reservoirs with devastating effect on both over wintered stockfish and resident fish alike.

When I look back at that period in the mid eighties the competitive name that was always there or thereabout in matches was Bob Draper from Northampton. He was possibly one of the first on the competition scene to use fast sinking lines and employ tactics that had never been witnessed before and that is in front of the drifting boat This has become an accepted and fruitful method in the present competitive scene married up to 'Blobs' and 'Boobies' although I have never witnessed a hatch of such like. Rules were brought to the fore that the rod held in the boat could not be pointed below the horizontal, lead core lines were debarred. Bob used to cast a fair line out and then plunge the rod down into the water up to six feet down before starting to retrieve, perfectly legal before the rules were adopted. That however did not interfere with my style of fishing which was a short line making good use of the wave and bobbing the top dropper in a team of four flies back towards the boat. Takes would be fierce affairs the trout would come from the depths over the fly, disappearing in a flurry of spray. The sight of that happening in the wave was like a magical drug to me and still is, especially so on the wild lakes that I fish. Whilst I also fished the dry fly and nymphs, my main method of attack was with the wet fly fished in what I term to be the age old traditional style from a boat drifting broadside on. Drogues were not allowed and most of the fishing was in the surface layers.

We travelled up to Orkney in a nineteen seater Mini Bus and crossed on the 'Ola' from Scrabster past the 'Old man of Hoy' to Stromness where we were based at the Stromness Hotel. When I tell you that the Loch of Harray is the utopia of waters for Brown Trout in the Northern hemisphere, it is an understatement. It was everything that I had dreamed of - skerry strewn, shallow, rich and productive. There was a very warm welcome from the Orcadians and we practiced for five days preceding the match on August 20th. On the Wednesday the team took a break from Harray and went to Loch Swanney. I however stayed on Harray and went out with the welsh team captain Cliff Harvey, a master at top of the water style of fishing with a team of wet flies. That day was a learning curve that will never leave me, Cliff angled his cast out across the wave and lifted the rod up allowing the following wind to put a forward bow in the fly line, now this method ensured that the fly line came off the water almost as soon as it had been cast out and that the flies were pulled behind it with and across the wave action in front of the drifting boat. The only thing facing the fish was the team of flies with the added bonus that if a fish showed, there was no retrieve but the flies lifted off and placed into the area, very quickly. Cliff used a Coch-y-Bonddu to great effect that day, If memory serves me right he accounted for over thirty trout under the fine boating skills of Billy Stanger, I also managed a decent bag of fish, most of which were returned to the water.

Billy Stanger looked after me on three days that week, a gentleman with exceptional knowledge of Loch Harray, with an unhurried manner about him that spilled out calmness into the boat so crucial in setting the mind to work and think in the right fashion. The boat was never quiet with a constant conversation either with my boat partner or myself. I can say with sincerity that during those three days in his company, Billy set my mind ready for the ensuing International Match.

When the Orkney Trout Fishing Association did the draw for the partners and boatmen I was teamed with a seasoned Scottish International and our boatman was to be the late Eoin McDonald. Eoin had a clinker built fourteen foot boat and a two horsepower seagull engine, not built for speed but would hold the wave and drift slower than some of the fibreglass boats being used, some with 9 horsepower engines.

It was crucial to make the right decision and although it was a long way off from the mooring and starting point for the match, both of us agreed that Josey's Bay would be a good plan. Eoin agreed. All the boats left the mooring just before 10am and as we motored out into a buoyed off area in the bay in front of the Clubhouse, a lone piper with his bagpipes was stood on the end of the stone pier, the pressure upon me brought tears to my eyes, and I turned to face the bow of the boat so that my boat partner and Eoin couldn't see me. I can't really explain that feeling in me, I just filled up , I couldn't help but think back to the days that I had lifted myself up to look over the edge at the fish on the draining board at home and my mother making me that first fishing rod, that first trout from the 'Wen', right through and back to my present position representing my Country a sort of a mind race in time.

My Scottish boat partner said that he had fished five times in the International team and had never been beaten in a boat, maybe it was a ploy to break my thoughts, unnerve me? A shotgun fired on the bank was our key to the start of the match and boats went off in different directions. We chugged along nicely downwind in a nice wave and the high cloud cover opened into brilliant sunshine, not exactly exceptional fishing conditions. I had tied four flies before breakfast, a Size 12 Gold Invicta for the point, a size 12 Haul-a-Gwynt variant for the first dropper, a size 10 York Special for the second dropper and a size 10 Coch-y-Bonddu for the top dropper, (Page 197/198/204) I had spares too, already on casts made up as time would be of great essence if something went wrong, which, of course it did! Half way down the Loch we drove into some Canadian pondweed and the engine choked up and stopped. As the boat came to a stop and came round into a drifting position, I noticed a deep hole within the shallows up ahead and asked if I could fish whilst Eoin sorted the engine out. Since my co-competitor had chosen to fish from the stern, I was in the bow, the reply was in the affirmative and the first cast, with the rod lifted to create that bow, brought the 'Coch' to the surface in a nice drift. Sweet as anything a trout came over it and I was in. I had him netted and in the bag in quick time and away again whilst my co competitor set about to start fishing. Next cast same again and two fish in the bag when Eoin started the engine and took us the remainder of the journey to Josey's Bay.

On our arrival, other boats covered most of the Skerry edges. By this time the boat was very quiet and Eoin nudged me and winked as he took on the oars in the central position in the boat. The remainder of the day is sketchy in my mind, but I recall drifting out across deeper water near to patches of pondweed and catching a number of fish between us. By the time we ended up back in the buoyed area in front of the Clubhouse, I had seven "measuring" trout to my co-competitor's four. We had returned a number of fish below measure. We had a few minutes left and started to fish drifting onto a skerry. In and amongst other boats, a fish rose to the Scotsman's fly and he missed it. The fish was half way down the boat, just on the boundary between and about ten yards out, so quick as a flash, as he gathered his line back after the missed strike, I was onto it and up it came again and hammered the Coch-y-Bonddu on the top dropper. A great trout of about twelve inches, an aggressive comment was made from the other end of the boat, as soon as I bent the rod into the trout 'That was my fish' and Eoin replied, that he'd had his chance and missed it. He winked again at me and smiled as I netted the trout and bagged it. On the shore there was a buzz with the team captains going around their respective teams to make a quick count of the numbers of fish. When he came to me and I said eight, his face lit up with delight. He'd only managed five to his own rod, but Cliff Harvey is that type of person that was very pleased with my return. No jealous small-mindedness from him. He knew that you have to be in the right place at the right time and doing the right thing.

79

As the weigh in commenced, Moc Morgan the Welsh team manager came up to me and said, that there was a few rods with seven but he hadn't heard of any with eight. He also mentioned 'Brown Bowl catch', When my turn came to weigh in Stan Headly poured the bag out onto the scales and said "seven trout for…", I interrupted telling him there were eight and for a moment thought I'd miscounted. He counted them again and said seven. "Check the bag Stan" was my reply, and sure enough, there was the eighth, stuck in the wet sacking. Phew, relief, eight trout for five pounds thirteen ounces an average of nearly 12 oz. (Page 100) There then followed an incredible period of anxiety as the rest of the teams weighed in and the announcement of the weights. Some anglers were approaching me and patting me on the back giving the thumbs up signal. These were intense moments until the announcement that the Scottish Team had won the match with 45 trout weighing 31lb 4oz, Ireland were second with 46 Trout weighing 29lb 5oz, Wales third with 37 trout weighing 25lb 1oz and England last with 38 trout weighing 24lb 8oz. Heaviest basket Gwilym Hughes, Wales. I had just won The Brown Bowl!, my boat partner for the day was the first to shake my hand and congratulate me.

It was a great evening at the Stromness Hotel, collecting the most prestigious and sought after award in International Lake Fly fishing competition. The 'Brown Bowl' was mine and I just couldn't believe it. (Page 99) The phone calls back to Wales that evening could well be described as the end of a particular journey in life, whilst it can throw all kinds of obstacles at you, it can also provide great moments. Is there an element of luck in fly-fishing? Of course there is, is there skill involved? Of course there is, all combined with dedication and total concentration, right time, right place, doing the right thing with skill and some luck thrown in. That's how it works, simple as that!

1983 was an incredible year for me as it involved a total of nine lake fishing competitions in all - from local clubs, Police force, regional, national and, international matches. The incredible part was that I took the heaviest basket of fish in every one of them. Hardy Brother's rewarded me with a certificate and a gold badge bearing 'Hardy Hall of Fame'. I don't polish it every day, only once a week. (Plate 2 Page 103).

Between 1983 and 1987 I represented Wales at International level in seven lake matches starting on the Loch of Harray, Lough Conn, Llyn Brenig, again Loch Harray, Lough Conn, Llyn Trawsfynydd and captained the team at Loch Leven, gaining two gold medals. These matches together with all the others I was involved in outside the International scene were quite heavy going and as I had fulfilled my ambition in all ways including to captain Wales, I decided to give the international scene a break.

I made a few visits back to Orkney over the years and nothing changes on the Island. The fishing is awesome. My latest visit was in 2005, which saw me back at Loch Harray, this time as a guest of Billy and Claire Stanger, celebrating the 100th anniversary of the Orkney Trout Fishing Association, absolute magic.

A Double 'Sting' and 'Bugging'

I enjoyed the relaxed atmosphere away from the International competitive scene. I continued to fish in the Police matches and recall an incident that occurred on a visit to Chew Valley Lake in one of the matches.

A group of us had travelled from North Wales early in the morning, to fish at Chew Valley a practice session before a match the following day. After the fishing we travelled to the 'Live and Let Live', a pub who catered for Anglers, near to Blagdon Lake, someone had arranged our stay there for the night. It was cosy and welcoming.

After a meal, we retired to the bar. Memory fails me as to every person that was part of that group I was in but I remember that Dave Gumbley and Colin Midgley were there. Whist in the bar area we broke into conversation with a group of Scottish anglers who had travelled to fish Blagdon and as the evening wore on and the beer flowed, I got talking about various Scottish locations I had fished - flies, methods and the like. I took a toilet break and upon my return into the bar one of the Scottish lads moved a chair for me to sit on the other side of the table and asked me 'Are you alright there?' He repeated it a couple of times during the next half hour or so, I was, and told him so, continuing with the conversation about fishing locations and the like.

Dave Gumbley and Colin Midgley got up to play pool and one by one the Scottish lads drifted away from the table we were sat at. I also had a game of pool and came back to sit down One of the Scottish lads brought me a pint and asked again if I was all right. I thanked him for the pint confirmed I was fine and started conversing with him again but this was short lived as the Scottish lads left the bar and I joined Colin and Dave by the pool table. We retired to our beds and breakfast was booked for eight o clock the next morning.

In the breakfast room we were first in closely followed by the Scottish lads. We bid them the pleasantries and one of them said to me "Nice fly box you have there". I was bewildered but Colin and Dave burst into laughter and I was more confused and said "What fly box?" and accused Colin and Dave of going into my fishing bag in the room and showing my fly box off without my permission. I can tell you that I was not well pleased with them and this must have shown in my expression. The laughing became uncontrollable and tears were flowing down their faces to the extent that they had to leave the breakfast room. One of the Scotsmen asked me from their table 'Are you OK mate? I just shook my head to indicate that I was and then shook it from side to side in disbelief at my team mates - what could they have been thinking of? How could my team mates have been so unkind as to show my fly box - at that time there were some personal patterns which I regarded as secrets of my own in there?

Colin Midgley returned first followed by Dave Gumbley, who was carrying a wooden fly box, which he placed on the table before me. It wasn't mine and they explained that unbeknown to me, Dave Gumbley happened to have been in the toilet before I went that previous evening together with one of the Scotsmen from our table. The Scotsman had told Dave that he was impressed with my knowledge and Dave had replied not to take too much heed of what I said and that I had been retired from the Police with mental health problems, that I read all the magazines and just related what I'd read. Also that I'd never been anywhere outside North Wales and that they had felt sorry for me and brought me down from the hospital just to give me a break. Dave asked the Scot to promise not to say anything to me, which he did, not a word, not a word. On his return to the bar, Dave let Colin in on the 'sting'.

When I went to the toilet and to put meat on Dave's story, Colin had picked a wooden fly box up from behind the bar, the 'Pub' fly box. It was full of incredibly untidy tied flies, some monstrosities, including sea flies and rusty spinners, tangled casts and the like, an opened up condom tied onto a hook was also among the mess. They presented it to the Scottish lads as my fly box and they believed. I took one look in the fly box and closed it. They explained the 'sting' and there was good-humoured laughter all around.

Now that side of the competitive scene never seems to be reported on does it and it happens constantly. Its not all fishing, fishing, fishing, win, win ,win. You meet up with an interesting variety of people and share stories, experiences in angling. Long may that continue. I wonder if that old box still takes pride of place on the bar of the 'Live and Let Live'? The Scottish lads also saw the funny side of it and when I now think back to the incident I sometimes wonder if they thought that we were all on release from hospital.

That day on 'Chew Valley' I blanked. So much for what I learned in practice and those personal flies - that's competitive fishing for you. You have to take the rough with the smooth - one day you can be right on top just to find yourself at the bottom of the heap the next.

1990 saw the Fips Mouche World Championship on the River Dee and Llyn Brenig. I decided to go and watch one of the sessions on the River. I had fished for Grayling in the winter months with weighted nymphs and fished for them with a fast sinking line in deeper slower pools in the middle reaches, with limited success. My favourite fly was a weighted Pheasant Tail Nymph.

What I saw that day in the World Championship changed my whole outlook and whetted the appetite again. I witnessed a Polish competitor proceed to take a dozen or so Grayling in quick succession from around his feet near a fast run. I watched closely and it was some time later that I realised how he had created a situation for the Grayling to come on the feed through his approach.

There was a narrow tumbling run of very fast water under and alongside the bank, which quietened and settled into a small pool at the head of a much larger and deeper pool. The river Dee at this point is quite wide, but he only used quarter of the width of the river, which was no more than twenty yards in length. He had about a foot of fly line out through the tip of the rod and a three fly cast with some seriously heavy nymphs on. I could almost liken his style to my father's with the fly rod and a worm in a flood, only much faster due to the fast water he was in. This was in clear water not coloured water and no more than a few feet away from him. I knew immediately that this warranted some serious thought and analysing by yours truly.

He went in at the top of the run and waded through it right up to the top of his chest waders. There was a pile of debris, leaves and sticks caught on a rock near the bank, the water just below the rock being packed solid with this debris. He stepped onto this and trod on it setting his feet right at the edge, then jumped both feet together straight into three feet of water and when I say fast water I mean fast, you would not wade through it in normal circumstances. This resulted in him being carried down by the current and he rushed quickly through to shallower slower water where he would spin around and fish into water he had waded through. He quickly worked down maybe five yards, or ten yards on some occasions, until he caught a fish and then waded back up. Now coming back he would wade more slowly and out into the river moving upstream twenty to twenty five yards, onto the glide in the pool above in one foot of water and present his fish to the controller, on the bank there. As soon as the fish had been measured and released in to the pool above, he would quickly walk down the bank again and wade through the very fast water and repeat exactly what he had done before. At the time I could not understand why he did not take the easy option of the wading he had done to bring the fish in to the controller, in shallower, slower water, further out, it just did not make sense.

At the end of that session it was the end of the match, I spoke to him and the controller. He had great difficulty conversing in English, so I could not get the complete answers to the mysteries of what he was doing. I did make out however that he was thrilled with the River Dee.

I saw on the marking sheet that he had caught sixteen fish in just over an hour. He showed me his flies; woven bugs on size 10 hooks. I walked back up to the car park with him at the end of the day, his clothing was dripping wet, and the controller told me that before my arrival he had been over the top of his chest waders a number of occasions that afternoon.

I spent the next few days going over and over in my mind his style of approach but could not grasp the basic concept of approach in my mind. I needed the answer so; in the end I went and tried it myself. Needless to say, I went straight in head over heels, good job it was a warm day. So on my next visit to the river I went to the very spot that he had caught the fish in and checked the depth right through using my rod tip - well I wasn't going to jump into that current. You could not hold the rod straight down such was the force where he had been going in. Obviously, more thought was needed.

Along and quite close to the bank there was a deep channel that led into a slower deeper pool and out towards the middle the river bed became shallower and gravely. I sat on the pile of twigs and had my feet hanging off the edge into the current. I picked a twig out of the pile in the river and to my amazement there was the answer, there were cased caddis, 'Grannom' sticking out everywhere from it. So the treading on the twigs was to release some of these and the fast wading in the rough water was to create a turbulence of aquatic insects to dislodge and be carried on the current downstream, bringing the fish from the pool below into the run to feed. So simple yet so wonderfully innovative a style - making use of the rivers' course and its aquatic contents to the full. After that preparation, all that needed to be done then was to present the nymphs and control them at the appropriate depth.

I had learnt something new by just taking a little time to reflect and analyse. Now the Polish angler was not 'shuffling' his feet whilst wading and disturbing the riverbed as he went, he just moved very quickly when he did, which possibly has the same effect. Another aspect to the approach was that his feet were never still for more than a few seconds. Right, I had something to work on and hopeful would enhance my success through the use of the new technique of 'bugging'.

When I went out in the height of summer or got onto a pool or piece of water that was not conducive to the 'Bugging' style of presentation and there was a hatch on I would fish with dries or small nymphs and sometimes both together fine tuning the art of upstream and downstream presentation. I would fish with a dry almost any time if the type of water in front of me warranted that approach, hatch or not and surprised myself in securing the odd fish in what appeared to be barren water.

Over the next year I practiced the art of presentation and moving through a pool quickly but thoroughly. It did pay dividends, I was catching more and more Grayling with this method of 'Bugging' and at my first attempt in a Welsh Salmon and Trout Association qualifier I secured my place in the International River's team. So I was back in to the International scene having had a break of six years. I did fish at Llyn Brenig and travelled to Rutland, Grafham and Draycote every year for an outing, but the same drive for the competitive side of lake fishing wasn't with me anymore, the river was the draw now.

The River Internationals

My first match took me to the River Wharfe above Bolton Abbey after which I qualified on six consecutive years - taking me to the River Tweed, River Agivey, River Dee, River Wye, back to the River Tweed and then to the River Liffey in Ireland.

I captained the Welsh team on the River Tweed in 1994 but it was in 1997 that the first Gold medal came on the River Wye in Derbyshire, followed by another on the River Tweed in Scotland in 1998.

In the River's International matches, a team of five anglers represent each of the four home countries, each Country run eliminating matches for qualification purposes and whilst there is complete harmony and friendship among the competitors away from the river, it is battle time as soon as the match starts.

You are drawn into a group of four anglers, one representing each of the home countries. The river section is separated into five beats of up to a mile in length. You are then drawn two beats which you and your group will fish. The day is split into four one and a half hour sessions, effectively making it four separate matches, fishing two sessions on one beat and then moving to another beat for the afternoon two sessions. Starting points are drawn also on the respective beats but after the start you can go anywhere on that beat provided you do not fish within thirty yards of another competitor. In-between sessions you have to move thirty yards. The scoring system is on the numbers of fish per session and their measurements, points for catching and points added for the length - each fish measured has to be above 20cm. These are totalled up and added to the team's performance overall and of course determine individual placing, the highest score securing 1 place point on your beat with the lowest score receiving 4 place points - a blank representing the lowest place points also. The lower number of place points at the end of the four sessions both singly and collectively in the team wins the match. At the end of the day and after four sessions on the five sections the marking cards are brought together and the place points added up. In the event of a tie on place points it is then down to the points scored by each angler, the number of fish caught with the largest fish representing the better angler and thus securing the better position, complicated but fair.

The River Tweed in Scotland is renowned for its exceptional quality as a Salmon River but little is said about the Sea trout runs, which are also prolific although I have never fished for them there at night. The Brown Trout and Grayling fishing is also exceptional and it is the 1998 International match that sticks out vividly in my mind, for more reasons than one.

The Welsh team had returned impressive results in the practice sessions preceding the match and the draw was made for the beats and starting points. In every match I have fished I have experienced that dry mouth at the start of the competition, whatever causes it. In practice I had witnessed a sporadic hatch of Blue Winged Olives on one of the beats and had spent considerable time with fish feeding on them, in and amongst some ranunclus weeds in three feet of water on a glide. I had discovered over time whilst wading through the weeded areas of rivers that the flowing ranunculus weed is a great holding area for trout and the weeds themselves for insects. Although when looking from above it would appear to be a solid mass, it really isn't for within and beneath what we see flowing back and to and side to side on the surface of the current are tunnels sometimes a yard or so in diameter and many more yards in length. Within these tunnels lie the trout and grayling, being out of sight and also close to their food source. Sometimes the weed separates on the current and you can see down to the riverbed in the right kind of light conditions. I had covered these rising fish with every fly pattern that I could think of and failed miserably to connect to any. You could see the Blue Wings floating downstream and you could see rises in the weed, but not a single take in over an hour. I returned to the car to reflect on this and had my lunch. I was totally bewildered as to what these fish were taking, I followed this with nymphing tactics and caught one trout and lost another, but when you witness a rise of fish in a small area and you can't catch them, something has to be wrong with the fly or the presentation or something else – whatever, it needed to be solved.

I had read of the great Canon William Greenwell who is famously known for the 'Greenwells Glory', and I'd tried the pattern, as it was initially sourced on the Tweed. The Canon had caught a natural insect possibly a Blue Wing and given it to a person called 'Brown' a headmaster and the natural handed to a professional fly dresser from Sprouston in Roxburghshire. He copied the body of the insect by rubbing dark cobblers wax into crimson yellow tying silk to form the body, leaving that olive hue that I have not seen matched by the dyeing process. They used that method back in the 1860's. Well, it didn't work that day. I put the rod on the bank and waded back into the river into a slower area of the weeds and sat on a stone near to where I had seen a fish rise several times and watched from a couple of feet away. I could see hordes of Blue wings floating down and suddenly noticed that none of the rises were actually on the hatched insect. Further observation of this saw that the fish were taking something just in the surface film, sometimes an inch or so from a hatched Blue Wing floating downstream. That hour spent on that stone was to prove crucial.

I returned to the hotel and in the meeting that evening, discussed this with my team mates. We all had something to throw in the pot with various experiences during the day. I set about to tie a fly on the basis of the Greenwell's Glory, but one that would have the body just under the surface film when floating down in a dead drift fashion. I used yellow tying silk rubbed through cobblers wax on a size 16 Mustad 80250 hook which has a curved shank. Over this along and above the hook shank, protruding out slightly past the bend of the hook I used a few strands of deer hair tips which when tied in splayed slightly and over the deer hair four natural coloured cul-de-canard feathers, set slightly shorter in length than the deer hair. These are the feathers which are found around the preen gland of a wild duck showing that blue hue. This dressing of the actual finished fly is what is termed today as 'F' fly style. The deer hair served three purposes, it was slightly buoyant, they had the appearance of legs when viewed from underneath the finished fly and held the cul-de-canard feathers in place off the hook shank ensuring that the body would be just below or in the surface film. Later I gave the fly a name, the 'Cul-de-Canon' (Page 180) I also tied some 'Bugs' to copy what other members of the team had found to be successful on the Grayling.

The next day I was back on the river and 'Bugging' away with some limited success when there appeared a hatch of Blue wings again, the trout in and among the ranunclus weed started to rise and I quickly changed to a dry and put the new creation to the test. Three casts and three fish was proof enough, the little emerger was what they were on. No wonder that they refused the dry version the previous day and a lesson was learnt from that observation that it was critical to not only present the offering in the right fashion, but in exactly the right place – in this case it was in the surface film at the right depth – a difference of millimetres!

That following day I walked my drawn beats, making mental notes of lies whilst the rest of the day was spent tying up a supply of flies for the team and also preparation of the tackle for the match day. I always was methodical about this, having spare casts ready made up in a wallet with flies attached and ensuring that everything else was up to scratch. Time is of essence in a match, right up to the last minute in each session and if I had a tangle I would have the cast off in seconds and another on. You will not catch fish unless your flies are swimming

My first beat was above the Dryburgh Abbey Hotel (Dryburgh North) - a lovely piece of the river very wide and quite slow and featureless in parts, but I knew that it held fish. I started right at the top of the beat and went straight in with some 'bugs' into a very likely looking run. Half an hour went by and a few Salmon Parr only - nothing else wanted to play so I decided to move downstream onto slower water and look for some activity. Only an hour left in the first session. On my way down I thought I detected a small rise almost on the far bank, just a small break in the surface on some flat featureless water, so I stopped and waded in with my other rod with the emerger pattern on. I cast over where I thought the fish had shown and covered that lie three or four times and as I was doing so through the corner of my eye, saw a fin break the surface slightly further up in midstream. I hauled excess line in quickly and covered it; sweet as anything the Cul-de-Canon was sucked down, not a blemish on the water surface. I lifted and was into a lively brown trout, which gave a good account of itself, jumping clear of the water two or three times before I netted it. It was measured and returned.

Now that first fish in a match is a leveller after which you settle, become calmer and start thinking on the positive side. I managed another three brown trout from that very long pool, and saw two Salmon show. At the end of the session I was quite happy with the four fish I had taken, not a rise, just fishing blind with an emerger both upstream and downstream drifts., seeking out area's where suds were present and dropping the fly within these. As I came out of the river at the end of the first session a salmon angler appeared from below and we exchanged pleasantries. I pointed out where I had seen the two salmon show and in return he told me that right on the lip out of the pool some one hundred yards away he had seen a trout move, where he had been fishing for Salmon. I went to the spot and saw a rise, two, three across the tail end in the last ten yards of the pool. I then caught another four fish to the Cul-de-Canon, down-streaming the fly to them in that second session. Presentation was a problem here as the water was faster just above the fall out of the pool. The result pleased me, as it was bright sunshine and very warm by that time, not good fishing conditions by any standard. The Salmon angler had re appeared towards the end of the second session unbeknown to me and was sat on the bank watching me and talking to my controller. When I came ashore, he had two fine fish - a Grilse and a Sea trout of about 7lb. He thanked me for the information and stated that I was pinpoint accurate with their locations.

I had not seen any of the other competitors on the section and was worried that the river may have fished better in the shade of trees further downstream but when I met up with them in the car park it was not the case, I had done well, so away we went for lunch with two session to go. When we all sat for lunch on the nearby village green, there was a lot of bustle and stories. One of the Welsh lads, Geoff Thompson, had seventeen trout in the first session and some more fish in the second - a great performance. The others in the team had also fared reasonably well.

In the afternoon I was to start with the beat that Geoff had been on, Edgar George the team coach and Moc Morgan the team manager were pleased with the result. Iwan Lewis on his beat had stuck to 'Bugs' in fast water and all his fish had been 'Grayling'. So off we went to the river knowing that if we did well in the last two sessions we could be in with a chance.

My third and fourth sessions were at Rutherford, another great Salmon beat. Knowing where Geoff had fished and the style he had used in rough water, I decided to start off the first session with 'Bugs' in the same area, but after half an hour of nothing, I moved downstream onto a long glide out of the last pool. There was some sparse ranunclus weed and I tried again with the Cul-de-Canon. Although there were no fish showing at the time I somehow managed another four brown trout by the end of that third session.

As I went into the last session of the day, fish started to move here and there, what I call 'oncers', up and down and I moved about here and there on the pool, catching three of them. There was only about half an hour left when I noticed a fish steadily rising in an eddy towards the faster water near to the run into the pool. I covered it and to my astonishment hooked into my best fish of the day, another brown trout. It was no easy task to get it to the net, but I managed and it went 43 cm. I was soon back in the pool and fished a downstream dry over a submerged ranunclus bed and I was in with the first cast again, the fish felt similarly heavy to the last one caught. It was way out across the river and it went deep and didn't show itself. Eventually after some side strain I got it into my half of the river, and near to my feet in four foot of water. Again the fish ran line off the reel and this time went straight into the ranunclus. where I could see it flashing about in the sunlight. I quickly made my mind up to go and get it and went in over the top of my chest waders and plunged the net down under it and lifted. It was my day, the fish was in the net and the weed broke away with it. I half swam ashore and got there about 1 minute to the end of the session. The trout measured 44.5 cm. I then lay out on the bank as, to be honest, I was exhausted from the effort I had put in during the day. I turned my feet around above me and lay sloping down and back towards the river, for the water to run out of my waders. I took one of those moments where I was looking up to the sky without a thought and then into my mind came the numbers - four, four, four and five - quite consistent over the sessions.

On arrival back at the hotel not all the cards were in but from the conversations and buzz I knew the Welsh Team had done well and that the 'Gold' medal would possibly be ours, we didn't have to wait long, 'Wales for the Gold, Gwilym Hughes International Rivers Champion and largest fish - a clean sweep'. I was elated, emotional and proud all at once – there's no way of describing in words the feelings of that moment. The Welsh team were bouncing around, Geoff Thompson who had returned that great catch of trout in the first session had a nightmare time on his afternoon beat blanking on one of them. That's the way it goes and after downing a very well earned pint of beer he went away to shave a beard he had been wearing for very many years as he had promised himself he would do so if he eventually won 'Gold'. Most if not all the competitors came to me and congratulated me. Terry Morgan our team Captain that year wore a constant smile that said it all and Gavin Jehu was just shaking his head in disbelief. If memory serves me right it was his first International. Iwan Lewis my close friend had stuck to the bugs all day, never caught a brown trout, all his fish were Grayling. It had been an in-depth team performance - in fact I would go as far as to say that it was probably the best prepared and technically capable team that I ever had the pleasure of fishing with. I say this with hand on heart - each one of them was capable of taking the Individual Champion position- it just happened to be my day, lady luck again. (Page 105).

That evening at the dinner I was made aware by one of the competitors, that I was the first person in the history of the home Internationals to have achieved the titles Rivers International Champion and Lakes International Champion. Again I felt overjoyed. By today that has been repeated by a young man from the North East of England, Simon Robertson whom I had the pleasure of watching during a particular International on the River Agivey. I was in the company of another great International angler, Jake Harvey of Scotland and I recall him saying to me as we watched him, 'Poetry in motion', Simon was, a very capable and dedicated competitor, he had a quality and flair about him far beyond his young years. I believe the double has also now been achieved by Jeremy Lucas from Cumbria - another truly great all round angler.

That night I proudly collected the 'Moc Morgan Trophy' and the 'Mike Childs' trophy for the largest fish with the added bonus of two great watercolour prints of the famous junction Pool and Bridge at Kelso, courtesy of another great Scottish International angler, Ronnie Glass.

My last Rivers International was on the River Liffey in County Kildare, Ireland in 1999 - a prolific easily waded river carrying a greater head of trout than I have experienced in any river ever. My qualification was automatic, after my success on the Tweed in 1998. I started off slow and then got it right for two sessions prior to losing three trout in quick succession on the last session. I still managed third place overall however which I was very pleased with. One of those trout that I lost on the final session would have put me back as International Champion for the second year running, but it was not to be.

Through personal choice I decided after that, that my time with the Rivers International as a competitor was over. In one way I was sad and in another pleased, for my life within angling was again on the change into another area. As a side note, I have been fishing the Liffey now each year since 1999 making two or three visits a year, and have made some very good friends - John Higgins, Nicky Moore and Kevin Somers all great anglers in their own right.

During the period between 1994 and 2004 I went to four of the Fips Mouche World Championship matches in the Czech Republic, Poland and Slovakia. as a competitor on three occasions, I did win a Bronze medal in the Czech competition, I think it was for the best catch of fish on a particular river over the whole of the match. Since I don't understand their language and I don't suppose they did mine I am guessing the reason. (Page 105) Nevertheless, it was still a medal and I was very pleased with it. My tally was twenty-six fish in three hours, nineteen wild browns, two grayling and five stocked rainbows, all from a two hundred yard stretch of water, on the 'bugs'.

During that trip I made some very good friends and learnt how to tie a proper Czech nymph, courtesy of Jaromir Sraam and Martin Musil our Czech guides. My results in the other matches were, in two words 'complete failures', hey, that's fishing. My other world Championship was when I was invited to coach the Irish team in Lapland, a great event and a great bunch of lads who fished their hearts out and came I believe higher in team placing than Ireland ever had done before in this match - they were fourteenth out of twenty one teams. At that level it is hard, believe it. We learnt a lot that fortnight, all of us. Competitive fishing is for the younger generation, for as you approach sixty, the body slows up, it is not easy running in and out of the river maybe over twenty times in an hour and a half, sometimes in hairy conditions, that's a fact. Do I miss it? Well in a way I do, but there again on the other hand I don't and that in itself has to be the sign that the competitive element is there no longer. There's no point in going out there not being bothered whether you win. You fish in a competition to win. That does not mean that the competitive element does not strongly exist as far as the fish are concerned , that thankfully remains as sharp as ever. I like to concentrate now totally against the fish and not against fellow anglers, there is a big difference and we all go through various experiences in an angling life.

*A Salmon and three Seatrout from the Upper reaches
of the River Dwyfawr in 1976 (Page 64)*

*1982 at Llyn Brenig with the Welsh
Salmon and Trout Association Challenge Shield, from
left to right Mike Green, Mike Plack, myself and David Owen
(Page 73)*

*Presented with the 'Brown Bowl' at the Stromness
Hotel Orkney in 1983 (Page 80)*

*Police Athletic Association International Trophy 1983
(Page 80)*

*One of the proudest moments in my angling life arriving ashore on
Loch Harray with the winning catch 1983
(Page 80)*

'Some of the Trophies'

Twaite Shad off the River Usk 2007 (Page 222)

*'River Liffey Trout' almost beaches itself
chasing minnows into shallow water 2007
(Page 213)*

*Salmon and Trout Association
'STANIC'*

*Game Angling Instructors
Association 'GAIC'*

*Game Angling Instructors
Association 'APGAI'*

*Hardy Hall of Fame Badge
(Page 81)*

My father's Sea Fishing Rod for use off the Rocks

My first Bonefish at 'Peace and Plenty' in Great Exhuma (Page 218)

*Brown Trout from Lough Corrib on the static
Nymph / flat calm and bright sunshine (Page 159)*

Fips Mouche World Championship in the Czech Republic
(Page 96)

1998 International Welsh River's Team.
From the left Myself, Iwan Lewis, Terry Morgan (Captain),
Geoff Thompson, Gavin Jehu and Edgar George (Team Coach)
(Page 95)

Changing my life's course,
STANIC, APGAI

In 1994 my Police career as a Detective came to a sudden end. I suffered a Myocardial Infarction - one of the heart muscles had died on me. This put me in intensive care for seven days and then when I got home, I could hardly get up the stairs to the bedroom. It wasn't looking good.

When serious ill health arrives, a reality check is necessary. I realised that my whole lifestyle had to change. As time went on I did everything the doctor told me to. Walking to the top of the drive and fresh cool spring air was initially punishing on the body, but through sheer determination and the medication I overcame the shortness of breath and the angina that prevailed. I lost the excessive weight I had been carrying and in a couple of months I was walking normally - well I had a River's International match to attend in July in Scotland and I was the team captain. - I just had to get better!, My connection to Angling in its various guises proved a saviour, yet again.

I could not exert myself fully without intense pain in the chest and arms, and any sudden change in temperature took some getting used to. The electrics in the body are amazing and I could tell you twenty four hours before a frost that it was going to happen. That is how sensitive I became. I also had to contend with the fact that I would never be the same again and that difficult but real decisions had to be taken. Therefore I chose early retirement from the Police Service, which I had devoted most of my life to.

I moved to live in Corwen, an area which was more akin to the lifestyle of my childhood and youth, far more so than the bustle of town life. One thing was clear in my mind and that was I would never put myself in a situation again whereby stress would have a bearing on my health. I needed freedom to do what I liked, when I liked and that suited me. As a consequence my health improved, slowly but surely. It took a number of years through controlled daily routines with adding a little on as I could until I felt as normal as I thought possible in the circumstances, whilst still on medication.

Rarely now is there any form of pain or of feeling unwell from my condition, but I do not push myself. I think I know my limits and I firmly believe that fishing played a major part in my recovery. It was the one and only connection with my past that I hung on to dearly and my new situation and lifestyle also allowed me to fulfil my obsession for angling on a daily basis I was also now perfectly placed on the banks of the River Dee. Only one problem now exists and Jennifer Lady Newborough, hit the nail on the head, "Gwilym, there is rather too much of you". Yes like many I suffer with my feet, I can't seem to keep them out of the pantry.

Through the sedentary period of my recovery I spent considerable time fly tying - in fact I went through all my fly boxes and set myself a target to renew all the flies and tie them to perfection. Practice, practice, practice, not good enough, try again. By doing this I replenished thousands of flies and tied some new patterns developing skills through trial and error, in the main picking up points from books, magazines and the like.

I wrote articles for Trout Fisherman Magazine and did a little consultancy work for Lureflash International, including running and judging their Fly tying competition for a few years. I also wrote a substantial number of articles over the years for Fly Fishing and Fly tying Magazine. Through this and my fly tying demonstrations at Chatsworth Angling Fair and the Go fishing Exhibition at the NEC in Birmingham and it was at the NEC that I met up with some APGAI members of GAIA.

I was tying flies on the Salmon and Trout Association stand and they were running the casting clinic. Whilst I was quietly impressed with their casting abilities, they were certainly not impressed with mine, on reflection, neither was I by comparison to the skills they displayed. I was actually enjoying helping anglers to better their personal skills, and soon learned that every participant whatever their abilities improved through encouragement. This developed through the Fly Dresser Guild meetings where I travelled to various locations in the Country for evening time demonstrations.

I decided to have a go at the Salmon and Trout National Instructors Certificate which was a weekend course where you had to demonstrate your teaching skills in a presentation, together with being assessed in your casting skills. I had a go at each of the categories Fly dressing / Salmon / Trout. I got my badge (Page 103) with the fly dressing and failed miserably on the casting side, noted on my mark sheet, "No knowledge of rod holding, poor on all casts, tailing loops, roll cast ok, very poor double haul". In the written test General 27/30 Salmon 8/8 Trout 8/8 Fly dressing 6/8.

Not being a person to lie down in defeat, I arranged casting lessons with Gary Coxon, the rough edges were soon knocked off me and my mind set right on how the rod works. Through relentless practice, six months later I achieved my goal and added the Salmon and the Trout casting to my qualification. This was in the spring of 2000.

I didn't stop there, on a daily basis and weather permitting, I would have the rod out on the field in front of the house. In fact, casting took over from fishing for a while. Further lessons again just to tidy up some faults that were creeping in and by the time that the Go Fishing show at the NEC came round in 2001 I was fairly adequate with the single handed rod in all casts. I recall being congratulated on my STANIC qualification by a couple of the APGAI qualified demonstrators who were present.

In July 2001 after more practice and tuition, I went for GAIA, APGAI assessment in Trout and Fly dressing. I achieved both at the first attempt and received my 'Game Angling Instructors Association' APGAI badge (Page 103). I followed this in April 2002 with the Salmon Double handed casting. One thing for certain if you want something bad enough and you put the effort in, it is achievable, how many times have I heard, "Oh I wish I could cast like that", well with dedicated effort and practice you can. I do not regard myself as a great caster, but I certainly know how the fishing rod works.

The casts can all be taught in the same way but it is more effective to use different messages to get the facts to register with people even though the rod only works in one way.

The Salmon and Trout Association moved with the times and formed part of the Angling Development board as the Governing body for Game Angling. The STANIC courses gave way to a new qualification, UKCC Level 2 Certificate in Coaching Angling. During the same period the 'Game Angling Instructors Association' opened their doors and extended membership to the new Level 2 CCA, STANIC and SGAIC qualified Instructors. As the STANIC qualification was no longer available through the Salmon and Trout Association, although still valid to those who held that qualification , the Game Angling Instructors Association created the GAIC Certificate, (Game Angling Instructors Certificate) (Plate 2) the basic casting qualification that afforded membership to the Association and was also used alongside the Level 2 CCA qualification to standardise the technical capabilities of the new Level 2 Coaches on their casting skills.

The Level 2 Course was well structured and covered Child Protection and Good Practice, First Aid, Risk Assessment and various coaching exercises. This, together with a portfolio of lesson plans and assessed coaching skills with the addition of the GAIA, GAIC fishing and casting skills, was far superior to the old STANIC course that I had attended, two years earlier.

My qualifications provided me with an opportunity to set up a business in Game Angling Instruction. I became active in converting my experiences into constructive coaching and instruction mainly on fishing techniques and approach in the varying conditions, with some casting thrown in where necessary. I became a Coach Tutor for the Level 2 CCA courses and External assessor and Verifier for the courses within 1st4Sport, Sports Coach UK. I was invited to coach at national level in Wales by the 'Welsh Salmon and Trout Association' and looked after the Ladies International Team for four years. Due to my other commitments I was unable to give this role all my attention and after four years withdrew from that duty in 2005.

I'm unsure who 'they' are but 'they' do say that you should experience everything in life once, I am certain that I do not wish to follow that advice in the true letter of the word, but as far as fishing goes then I do want to experience all of it within reason in its various guises and have something to offer a newcomer to the sport right through now to the advanced techniques. We must never ever think that we know it all, or become complacent in our approach to any situation in angling for if we do we shall fall heavily. There is no better leveller than angling and it is important to have an approach which allows one to continue to learn on each outing and hopefully to pass on this information in one way or another for a long time to come.

I strive towards perfection if I can in any coaching situation, irrespective of the calibre and capabilities of the client involved. Satisfaction is achieved when that client is at his personal limit in that particular concept of the learning curve - when he can go away happy and develop on the grounding received during the coaching or instruction. Perfection in reality is never reached for there will always be something new around each corner and with each new outing or experience.

I get a small buzz these days when someone masters a simple technique and adds something that enhances their technique in any given situation.. Casting techniques has been covered in very many books and many Instructors specialise in that area. It is a continuously expanding shifting base as techniques develop and new ones emerge. Personally my approach is to try to impart some simple terms for the client to reflect upon within his / her own capabilities in casting techniques and allow the client to go on and develop them in practice. Let me try.

Let us think about a single handed rod and the simplicity with which it works – it is certainly not rocket science. When you hold the cork handle of the fly fishing rod in the palm of your hand and place your thumb along the top of the cork towards the point of the rod, think that wherever you move the rod handle to by moving your hand, the rod tip will follow in the direction the thumb is pointing. This is also the case with the rod tip and the line, for the line will follow the path of the rod tip. If you slightly break the wrist in a casting action it allows your thumb to move from side to side or even around in a circle action, the action is carried through to the rod tip but is much exaggerated there and if you follow that down the line from the rod tip, it multiplies further still. Half an inch wrong with the thumb movement spells disaster at the end of the line.

The rod under pressure bends like a spring and this pressure is created when you move the rod against the weight of the line whilst casting . When you stop that movement the spring straightens up again and the line will shoot in the direction the spring travels into before it stops, move it in the opposite direction and stop again and the line will follow in the opposite direction.

Let us picture a train on a railway track. If the track is buckled the likelihood is that it will derail – clearly we need an even track for the train to stay on course. If we transpose this thought and convert the train into the fly line and the rod in your hand into the track, what we need to do is to keep the track path level and straight and the line will travel straight, buckle the track in any way and the line will do the equivalent of derailing. So keep everything on a straight track in any direction you choose to bend the spring and the line will follow - it has no option

Within the concept of the above, rod tip follows thumb and the line follows the rod tip and if on the correct tracking it should work fine.

How much to bend the rod is proportional to the length of line out of the tip. The more the weight the more it will bend and the longer the line the longer it will take to straighten out. That means that you only need to bend the rod sufficiently to move the line on a straight path in the direction in which you want it to go. In turn you only need to pause for long enough after the stop for the line to open up before you move the rod and bend it in the opposite direction to send the line back where it came from initially. Watch the line carefully if it collapses then there is one reason which is the 'incorrect application of power – too little', if it bounces about then there is one reason 'incorrect application of power – too much'.

As I said, the power application required is gauged by the amount of weight of line out of the rod tip - the longer the line, the longer it will take to lift and travel through the air and the longer the pause to allow the line to pass the tip and straighten out before you replicate in the opposite direction. We are talking here of fractions of seconds.

Put all that together and you have a correctly applied cast. Take your time, give the rod time to load, don't try to rush or overpower it, it serves no useful purpose. Load it on an even straight track, take your thumb in the right direction and the rod tip and line will follow. If it goes wrong, watch your thumb on the rod hand, it will give you a clue as to what the fault is. That's it, good luck and please do not practice this with a fly on the line - use a piece of wool until you are competent.

If you analyse your casting and apply the basics described above, your casting will improve but if in doubt see a qualified Instructor, one that is accredited and certified so by a professional body, It will pay you in the end for your fishing will certainly be enhanced.

The insight into managing coaching skills and teaching made me view 'Coaching' in a different light and realised the value and potential of 'good coaching practice', whilst I did not loose sight of the fact that the technical issues were very important, the reality although not abundantly clear at the time was that I was keeping ahead of the game.

Whilst this was ongoing, I had met and made friends with Iwan Lewis, a 'natural' angler and it led to my coaching him in various technical skills, approach, presentation – with him eventually gaining his first Welsh International Cap. Iwan Lewis was already a keen and dedicated angler and a competitively spirited young man with a great talent. I identified certain area's and advised on how to put those talents and skills to his fullest advantage in a fishing situation, this benefitted him. I was able to help him along this route with my experience and the coaching skills that I had personally developed. It was, in fact, a learning curve for both of us, as is every coaching situation.

The result was that Iwan became Welsh Rivers National Champion in four successive years and was only narrowly beaten to second place in the Commonwealth Championship on the one occasion he entered. He is now a fully fledged Welsh International Angler and a great one at that. We often discuss tactical and presentation aspects and are constant fishing companions. To quote Iwan "I fly fished this river Dee for twenty five years, nineteen of them the wrong way until I met Gwilym Hughes" – that is kind of him because, as I said, he is a naturally gifted angler and a keen competitor.

My opinion, for what it is worth, is that Instruction or Coaching of any kind having seen the positive results many times over is very important to every participant, especially if you are not succeeding when others around you are. I also include myself in this evaluation as only two years ago I watched Steve a ghillie on the Caberston beat on the River Tweed use a fast sunk line technique to great effect in very high water, whilst I remained blank. I watched and learned and since returned to the beat with success, having practiced the same method. No you never stop learning and as with all things in life there will always be someone better than yourself at certain aspects - that you have to accept and be prepared to learn. I am always looking out for some new technique, material, method and the like. Nothing is too much and nothing too little because they can all be put in the memory's portfolio for those difficult days we are all likely to encounter.

I am often asked this question when in discussion with anglers, "Have you any new fly patterns?" and the pet reply is simple but true, after a short pause and a bewildered facial expression, "Is there any new trout food?"

Anglers who appear confused by the range of the qualifications often ask for an explanation regarding the different organizations out there, more often than not about AAPGAI. Let me explain the facts here for you about GAIA (Game Angling Instructors Association) and AAPGAI (Association of Advanced Game Angling In structors).

AAPGAI was formed in 2003 at the GAIA meeting at Caer Beris in Wales. It was formed for the specific purposes of those who held the APGAI qualification to come together socially and for skill development as a resource for GAIA, this all under the umbrella of GAIA. I was present at that meeting and it was Ian Moutter the Secretary of GAIA who proposed the formation and I voted in favour. It became clear very quickly that certain members of GAIA, who were also holders of the APGAI qualification were intent upon using the formation of AAPGAI to break away from the main organisation. Initially, these members attempted to force the thinking of a very few upon the majority, then they tried to gain control over the APGAI qualification. When these attempts proved futile and it was clear that GAIA was not willing, or indeed able to concede to their wishes, they effectively broke away and formed their own qualifications.

Some members of AAPGAI , sadly have attempted and continue to undermine GAIA and deliberately mislead people to this end. This possibly has been done to build up AAPGAI at the expense of the main organisation, GAIA. GAIA's answer to this, is and has been, to get on with the real work of promoting quality game angling instruction, developing the recognised qualifications GAIC and APGAI, both of which are wholly owned by GAIA and to look to the future of game angling instruction for all levels of recognised qualification.

As the professional body for game angling instructors in the UK, GAIA recognises that anyone has the right to form an Association, when AAPGAI broke away from GAIA those involved were fully entitled to do so. It should be clear, however, that GAIA represents the vast majority of instructors in the UK and is the sole owner and adminis trator of the APGAI qualification. It is also the body recognised by the governing body for Game Angling, the Salmon and Trout Association and also the Angling Development Board.

GAIA is continuing to develop its qualifications in the areas of coaching, game angling instruction and casting skill development. As such it is unique and of vital importance to the future of game angling instruction. GAIA is comfortable in others pursuing their own agendas, as the management of AAPGAI have done, but it should be clear that, no matter what anyone may claim, the historical APGAI qualification has nothing whatsoever to do with AAPGAI and that AAPGAI is a trade organisation of casting instructors, that issues its own qualifications to its members.

The claim that AAPGAI was formed to represent the APGAI qualified instructors, is completely misleading, at the time the majority of APGAI qualified instructors were members of GAIA. It is also clear that AAPGAI was originnally formed to serve the ongoing requirements of GAIA and its members, no matter what may be claimed by a few who choose otherwise. All this is minuted. Changes are again afoot relative to the Governing body for Game angling and who knows where this will lead?

I hope that this spells out the reality.

River Fishing Trout and Grayling

You should match your fishing tackle to the general size of the fish that you are likely to encounter and also the size of the river you are fishing in. With some methods you need to present your offering delicately, other methods not so. When fishing for trout or Grayling you may encounter fish from 20cm to 50cm in length, a few ounces in weight through to 4lb in weight. For such situations as a general all rounder, I would recommend a medium to fast action rod, some 9' or 9'6" in length, 5 or 6 weight. The length of rod will vary if fishing small streams under trees and the like when a 6', 7' to 8', 3 or 4 weight would be quite adequate and in fact better suited - married to a double taper or weight forward profiled floating line.

I find that these days I have no need for any kind of sinking line, generally, but there is one method that it lends itself to and that is mini lure fishing and for this I carry a fast sinking line. I pack my reels with sufficient backing to bring the line almost up to the rim, not only is this advisable it helps keep the line straighter, less coils within. Large arbour reels are very good as more length of backing is stored also. I use an arbour knot for the backing onto the reel drum - a simple overhand knot around the reel drum followed by a similar overhand knot around the backing running off your backing spool which when tightened, the knot around the drum will slip until the second knot comes into contact with the first knot. Tighten this and trim the surplus and wind on sufficient backing line.

I use a nail knot to attach the backing onto the fly line. Keep the fly line on its spool or a line winder when winding it onto the reel as this prevents the line from twisting. Run the whole line out on a lawn or field and re wind it back on making sure that there is no line twist. At the business end of the fly line I immerse the first 1" or so of line into acetate solution holding it there for about a minute. I then strip the plastic coating off the line core and tie in a double overhand knot, slipping this to within a quarter of an inch from the plastic coating at the end of the line before tightening up and trimming the surplus to within an eighth of an inch to the knot.

I do not use braided loops, I find them bulky and sometimes difficult to pull through the rod rings, especially so when you have a longish cast because when it comes in through the tip rings on the rod, it gets trapped. I like my line to slip through all the rings smoothly and effortlessly when pulling line off the reel or winding it on. If however you prefer a loop at the end of your fly line all you need to do is to strip some more of the coating off and create that loop in the braided core of the line.

The cast is another very important aspect of river fishing and to this I pay particular attention. I do not use the tailored tapered leaders as I find them unnecessary in actual fishing although great for casting demonstrations when that perfect turnover is required. I'll explain why later. I make mine up as I go along or pre prepare them if I know where I was going to be fishing. At the end of all my leaders I make a loop with an over hand knot, the loop being usually about 1" in length. Make a lasso with the leader and loop and slip this over the end of the fly line and tighten in on the line side of the small knot. It's very simple and effective and to remove it all you have to do is catch the leader loop and push it against the fly line core to open it up and it slips off. It is secure and very quick to change casts.

For the 'Dry fly' I use a leader of 4lb or 5lb breaking strain and on a medium to large river would ensure it was about 12' to 14' long. To the end of this I attach a piece of about 18" of finer material, but never less than 3lb breaking strain I work on the diameter aspect when selecting the fine tip. I join the two pieces together using a figure of eight knot, I find this easy to tie, it takes seconds, and it's totally reliable and carries no bulk. Simply catch 5" or so from the end of the cast and trap between finger and thumb, cross this point of contact with the finer tippet end leaving about 5" of the end of the tippet pointing in the other direction towards the main line. Catch these two pieces together towards the point of your leader and form a loop 2" to 3" in diameter trapping the loop between finger and thumb. Place the forefinger and middle finger of the other hand into the loop and twist the loop around twice, place the thumb and forefinger into the loop and trap the fine point and the end of your leader between finger and thumb and pull it through. Let go of the grip on the loop between finger and thumb and pull both double pieces apart slowly and you will notice a shape of a figure 8 forming. Wet this and pull together gently as there is no need to over tighten this knot. Let the fish do that against the rod tip because when you are fishing, you can be very confident about the strength of this knot. Indeed I have tried them all and found this the quickest and the strongest. Trim off the surplus and tie on your chosen fly.

I use the same knot to form wet fly leaders with level nylon when making up leaders / casts, trimming off just the piece pointing back towards the fly line and leaving the forward pointing one towards the end of the cast for the dropper. If you get a break off in the take, which does happen sometimes, you may have tightened the knot up too much in the first instance or the rod and line set up was in too direct a line towards the fish. To prove this try to break a leader knot at an angle off the tip of the rod. There are other scenarios when you can snap off in fish especially in the take but it does not happen often and it's not normally down to the tackle but down to the individual using it - striking too hard or the fish going one way you lifting in the opposite direction against it. Remember the strike or lift needs only be sufficient and quick enough to set the hook point.

At one time I was the world's worst for snapping off on the strike and resorted to using an expanding rubber bungee between the line and cast, until I realised that I had been over tightening my knots and weakening them in the process. You live and learn.

To set up a 'Bugging' leader is also quite simple. Using the same rod as for the dry fly with the floating line, make up a cast with a loop for joining onto the line and make up two droppers of equal distance apart using the same figure of eight knots. The three fly set up should be no more than 9' long.

To set up for a nymph in front of the 'Dry' simply shorten the 'Dry fly' leader to about 9' at the fly line end. Tie in a piece of fine 3lb nylon using a half blood knot onto the 'Dry fly' hook bend, to extend out beyond the 'Dry fly', length to suit the depth you wish the nymph to sink to, possibly no more than about three feet. This is known as the 'New Zealand' method. In colder weather in the spring and autumn I extend this to 4' beyond the 'Dry' and use two weighted nymphs to get them down more quickly to near the river bed - more about its use later.

I seldom use a team of wet flies in a down and across method for trout or grayling these days. I just stick to those leader set-ups described. Normally I have two rods set up, one with the bugs one with dries or dry and nymph in front. I sometimes have the nymph that will go below the 'Dry' tied onto a piece of 3' nylon in the fly patch on my fishing waistcoat so that I can quickly change if the need arises.

I use chest waders always these days, breathable in summer and neoprene in winter. I use a short wading jacket with a short fishing waistcoat over, just the short waistcoat over a shirt in the warm weather, a peaked cap, Polaroid glasses with a small magnifying lens in the base. I find that very useful when examining insects and the like on the bank. I carry a couple of boxes of flies, Bugs in one and nymphs and dries in the other, a cast wallet with spare casts made up, flies thereon, nylon, floatant, sinkant, snips, amadou drier patch , a wading staff, a small pan net on a coil carrier off the back of the wading jacket or fishing waistcoat, and wear a neck inflatable lifejacket. That's it, travel light and move often.

The approach is critical in any situation as you will need to give yourself the best chance possible for success. The best advice I was given very many years ago and still holds, is to sit on the bank some distance from the pool you intend to fish and give it a few minutes just watching the pool. You may notice rises, you will see if there are any insects about, you will note the current changes, where the rocks are in the pool and the deep holes and shallow glides.

This is not a hundred percent reliable in all cases but it is a template you should keep in mind on your approach. Imagine that this pool is a restaurant set on three floors with rows of tables running the length of the pool, the basement the middle floor and the top floor, you are the waiter and your menu is your fly boxes. In the main not all the tables will be occupied all of the time, neither do you have the ability often to see all along the middle floor and basement. If you tackle the pool like this, you would visit each of the tables in turn, you must be careful that minimal disturbance occurs, although sometimes three or four tables are visited in one cast. In some circumstances it will be down to stealth and in others not. Often you can walk almost on top of the fish, especially grayling, trout too where there is a lot of weed present. A good waiter moves his / her feet about the restaurant floors, is attentive to all needs and as a result will collect more in tips than the static inattentive waiter. I hear often, "they're not feeding today" - well when you look at the menu in a restaurant do you choose everything that is listed? No you would select what you fancy. In other words fish will feed most times but have to be convinced that the meal is good, so the presentation aspect comes in - would you accept a meal that didn't look right or presented in the right manner by the waiter? Think about Julie Walters as an old lady in her televised sketch delivering the 'soup' and spilling it on the way with the customers moving out of the way of her delivery route to the table, would you accept it?

Presenting a 'Dry' fly in the right manner to a fish is crucial. It is artificial and so the presentation of it needs to replicate the movement of the natural it is intended to copy. Let's imagine a natural 'Olive' floating downstream over the fish. In the main the fish will see it coming into its view and move towards it, sometimes it will drop back and come up to meet it as it passes, sip, and its gone, sometimes it will move off station across the pool to either side to intercept, before returning to its lie. You can be sure that the movement will be leisurely as they do not exert too much energy. That natural fly causes no problem as it will be following a path that the current presents, one that the trout or grayling will be accustomed to and any deviation from that path through the pool or chosen lie of your artificial offering can set the alarm bells ringing and a refusal of the artificial. How do we do this and how can we avoid the normal pitfalls of presenting an artificial? Well, there are several ways.

Angle your cast to cover the lie where it will least be affected by the current on the water surface - that can be upstream or downstream, up and across or down and across. The presentation of this needs to take into account that the water surface from under the rod tip may not be moving in the same fashion as it does over the lie whilst in between you have your line and your leader which could also cause presentation problems. In executing the cast prior to the line alighting on the water surface you can put in a reach, a reach mend, a slack line or a parachute cast to enable and allow the artificial offering to drift over the lie along the same path as a natural would take. Remember the natural is not attached to anything, whilst the artificial is. You certainly do not want a perfect turnover in the cast delivered that is a recipe for a refusal of the offering hence the reason I said earlier that I do not favour tapered leaders for actual fishing, the turnover is too perfect. Neither do you want the fish to see the line first as that could also lead to a refusal. This is the reason that the fly is on a leader of at least 12' to 14' length, sometimes longer, to account for irregular current movement in the pool chosen to fish in.   Executing such casts allows that short drift over the lie when the leader has not turned over fully in dead drift fashion. I like my leader to collapse in the cast. This can be imparted into the cast immediately after the stop on the forward cast by tapping the tip of the rod down towards the river surface or at any appropriate angle you wish to impart. Naturally the cast length would be shortened to suit if fishing a small brook.

You've selected an imitative pattern to match the hatch, covered the lie and the fish has refused twice, what do you do now, change the fly or think, is it not feeding any more? If your presentation has sent those alarm bells ringing the fish is better left alone until it starts to feed again. Think about that invisible drag in the artificial? But how can one see something that is invisible? Well, lets call it a micro drag then, when your fly alights on the water focus on a piece of flotsam nearby, either a small bubble a piece of weed or the miniature white froth bubbles in the surface film , the suds and watch both closely, in their downstream path. If they float down together without parting on the surface current, the presentation is right and nine times out of ten the fish will have a go at the artificial. If the bubble and fly do part in the drift then the presentation is wrong and the fish is unlikely to rise to your fly. This is usually the reason behind the refusal.

To overcome this, move your feet and angle the cast over the lie in a different fashion, it does not always work but more often than not it does. In fast turbulent water at the head of a pool or run you do not encounter this kind of problem often, but I still try to collapse the presentation for when the fish sucks it down the cast simply follows in an unrestricted fashion, which allows the fish to catch hold of the artificial more effectively. To execute this kind of presentation it only requires a slight movement of the rod tip. Indeed if you were standing on the bank watching me execute this, you would not notice it in the presentation such is the delicacy of it. It's not untidy, just practical and very effective and it turns half rises into solid takes.

What about when fish are rising steadily in a glide, you see the insects floating downstream, you have done everything as suggested to you and still there have been no takes. That surface film is a critical area in Dry fly fishing, when you see the fish breaking the surface and then refusing the high floating dry off the surface film, think again and look at the rise form. Is the snout breaking the surface film or is the tail of the fish creating that magical ring to show its presence? If it's the tail, it suggests that the insects of interest are those hanging in or just below the surface film, pre hatching or just crippled and unable to break though the surface tension. This is when your emerger type dry fly will come into its own, in the film or just below it. (Some persons who call themselves 'purists' do not regard emergers as dry flies but that is pure hair splitting) The parachute pattern allows the body of the artificial to be totally beneath that surface film and tension. As far as I'm concerned, each of these types can be categorised as 'Dries' and you could say, Fully Hackled Dry (right on top of the film); hackle trimmed along the underneath of the hook shank (slightly in but on top of the film); 'F' fly type using a curved shank hook (in the film but slightly underneath); 'Parachute' type (whilst the hackle and post sits on top the body is below the surface film) and; 'Shuttlecock' type (the body hangs under the surface film in a different position to the 'F' fly.

If you do not have each of these fly patterns I suggest that you acquisition a full set it will convert a mediocre day into a brilliant one. Also don't be afraid of ringing the changes as the fish can go off feeding below the film and come and take the full adult hatched on the surface. Sometimes its just like switching an electric light on off and you will need to be ahead of the game. Successful fishing is a thinking game not a chuck and chance it affair.

Do not miss out on a very good time of year. Whilst some anglers shy away from the rivers when they are full of leaves falling off the trees in the autumn, the Grayling can be very active on the surface, 'yes' the leaves as they die away curl up and this is a great hiding place for insects to shelter from the deteriorating weather patterns. When the leaves fall the insects and creepy crawlies come out of their hideaway onto the water surface and you can be sure that the fish know about this, some of my most memorable dry fly outings have been on such days.

During different times of the day and different times in the fishing season your aquatic insects present will become active in the pre hatch period. Remember that all of them begin their ascent to the hatching position in the surface film from the river bed and this could be from a number of feet down to just a few inches in depth. Those periods in the day, not a fish seems to stir at the surface, but that doesn't mean that they are not active. Stand on a bridge or a high vantage point above a pool glide and observe the water, those fish present are well camouflaged, keep watching and in the light from above you will see glints of their sides as they turn to intercept a nymph.

This is where the nymph below the 'Dry' method comes in to play. In fact there are two periods that are important to think about here. Firstly when the fish are topping, creating rings and refusing the dries and emergers in the surface film it could well be that the rings are caused by the tail or dorsal fin of the fish touching and cutting though the surface film as it turns down to take a nymph floating downstream, anything from a few inches deep to a foot or so below the surface. Secondly, when there is no surface activity at all and the fish are still on station they can be fished for in a blind manner using this method with the dry fly in this case being used as an indicator for the take on the nymph. So you have two possibilities in one cast, the fish could come and take the dry or it could take the nymph. - a double whammy method. The flies are cast upstream and allowed to drift back towards your position in dead drift fashion, the artificial nymph sinking is at the mercy of the current and would follow the path a natural nymph would take. In this instance you would approach the pool from below and fish it upstream, remember the restaurant, visit each table, follow the template, keep moving your feet, cover all the lines of tables and remember you are fishing now on the upper and middle floor at the same time. If the chosen menu item is right you will succeed. As soon as a fish touches the nymph the dry will dip below the surface and that's when you lift into the take.

In the colder days of the year in spring and autumn I use two weighted nymphs in front of the dry fly. For this method I increase the size of the dry to accommodate the extra weight. This method of dead drift presentation lends itself well to fishing slower and deeper pools, even in the depth of winter when shoaling grayling, will be attracted and sport can be fast and exciting once the shoal has been located, usually in the basement part of the restaurant. One very important presentation method to explore in the depth of winter is to allow the point fly on the set up to touch the bottom, preferably a gravelly bar within a slow moving pool in six to eight feet of water and allow it to rest there for a few seconds, lift the rod tip up in a small tapping motion, once, lifting the dry fly two or thee inches off the water surface and allow to drop down again and watch it closely takes will be soft and the dry will slide away slowly, tighten into each dip of the dry, you will be amazed for the method will secure you many Grayling, especially so in a located shoal, yes induced takes. This method of inducing a take will work in swift gravelly runs at other times of the year, with lighter and smaller nymphs, but one has to change the setup in order to fish further away, use a piece of thin 'braid' between the fly line and the cast this dispenses with the weight of the fly line out of the tip of the rod as it is held high and is easier controlled the braid will not be as eager to drop back towards you thus pulling the nymphs off the dead drift. I use a piece of about 12ft long and keep low in the approach, it is also advisable to use a lightweight 10ft or 11ft rod for the purpose for you can achieve a higher rise and angle thus affording you to fish further away. I have found also that during the winter months although the wild brown trout have left the main river and are in the tributaries going about their spawning business, the stocked triploid browns keep on feeding in the main river and become very silvery in colouration with only a few red spots. These are in prime condition and you know immediately when you've hooked one as they become very acrobatic in their quest to throw the hook. The best way to bring them under control is to plunge the rod tip down into the river and pull on the line, this seems to disorientate them and they come quietly to the net or for hand release. It may sound odd but you should have confidence in this I have never seen it fail.

This now leads me on to the other method I employ commonly referred to as 'Bugging'. The set up and approach here is different, with a team of three weighted nymphs - sometimes heavy weighted nymphs or a mixture of both - on a nine foot cast. You can either wade a pool downstream or upstream presenting the flies to the fish in a dead drift fashion in the main. The flies are allowed to drift at the mercy of the currents they encounter down below. Out of the tip of the rod comes about three feet of floating line and once you have waded into the pool and are confident that the current is strong enough to keep the nymphs moving through the pool, allow the bugs to trail behind and downstream of your position. Then the arm and rod are taken over in an arch shape similar to a roll cast but on a much wider arc placing the nymphs in a straight line out and upstream into the current where initially the nymphs are allowed to sink on their downstream dead drift. The arm is outstretched and rod pointing above the flies, the rod tip is lifted to straighten the line and cast, the point fly or both the point fly and first dropper are allowed to bounce downstream, the rod tip moving at the same speed as the current , with the rod tip in a downstream position to the following nymphs, the arm comes into the body as the nymphs come nearer and then outstretch again as they go past. The end of the fly line is held just in the water and at any falter of the line on its downstream movement, tighten, in a short sharp tap downstream and in towards your bank, it may be a stone and then again it may be a fish. The strike is aimed in this way so as not to lift the nymphs from the basement and middle floors of the restaurant. By outstretching your arm in the upstream movement and a slight swivel on your hips downstream as they pass through to the outstretched arm, you are able to control the depth better, the bugs should not be pulled against the current.

The nymphs fish past four tables in one showing whereas if you kept your arm into your body it will only go past two tables in one showing, the more tables you visit, the better your chances are. Now after two casts go to the next set of tables and search the whole pool out in this fashion, either moving downstream or upstream in your search. The takes are sometimes quite vicious and you will see the end of the fly line plunge or pull away and at other times the line just falters. You need to concentrate fully as this is sight fishing and you will not normally feel the take on the dead drift of the nymphs.

There is another type of take that you should be aware of and it was by sheer chance that I tightened into one of these and realised what was happening. I was fishing a pool on the river Dee in company with a number of other anglers. It was frosty and cold and I knew the run we were in held fish. I was the third to go in at the tail end of the run and work it upstream, the other two anglers who had fished it before had not contacted any fish. Neither had I and half way up the pool when I noticed in parts of the dead drift the fly line in contact with the water surface seemed to travel downstream quicker than the current for some reason. I watched for this closely and struck into the next instance of it happening and to my amazement it was a grayling. By the time I had reached the run into the top of that pool I'd taken eight grayling, each one to this kind of take.

To analyse this, the grayling were turning downstream after the bugs, mouthing them and spitting them out as quick as anything. The actual mouthing was indicated in the weight being taken off the line and hence the line speed increasing in a downstream movement, it was very minimal the movement but it was there and I have experienced it many times since, especially so in cold weather. I recall being asked once by an angler more than a few times in the space of an hour as he watched me catch fish with this method, "When do you actually strike?" I explained the faltering in the line on the water, and actually showed it happening at close quarters. Essentially the answer to the question is simple, "when the fish has the bug in its mouth" but "yes but how do you know?" Well after much practice it becomes instinctive, the fish do not hold the 'bug' in their hand do they?, he looked at me in a rather strange manner, what else could I say?

The 'bugging' method is enhanced when every third cast or so you actually allow the nymphs at the end of the dead drift below you as the line tightens up on the downstream current, to swing round and up through the middle to the upper floor. As it is coming up just tweak it slightly by moving the rod tip in 2" soft jerks, especially alongside a boulder or similar object where fish could lie up - against tree roots is another likely spot. With this added touch that the dead drifting bugs appear to come alive and the method could well be described as the final movement of the flies when the down and across method is adopted in presentation. This style of fishing with heavyweight 'Bugs' can be likened to the 'Yorkshire' style of fishing a team of 'spider' patterns, the comparison aspect relates to the 'dead drift' in the presentation aspect. With the 'spider' patterns more fly line is used out of the rod tip and the flies either roll cast or cast in the traditional overhead method, and the presentation due to the lightness of the flies is in the upper layers of water, also very effective at times and a style which should not be overlooked.

Always remember when wading upstream that you are disturbing the gravel and stones and dislodging food items as you go, grayling lock onto this and come in below you and feed on the morsels. This should not however be done deliberately as in shuffling the feet to create this effect. Wading can be a tricky affair at times, so you need to be wearing an inflatable life jacket, preferably an automatic one, tread carefully and move sideways against the current, crab fashion. It's the safest way especially so in heavy water as you will find that the force of the water is in the upper layers and its slower down below, so this could be putting pressure on your thighs from the knees up. A wading stick is also advisable and always try to look before you step, steadying one foot before you move the other.

The other method I employ with the 'bugs' is in areas that I can not reach through wading, I lengthen the line and cast conventionally overhead, being very careful using a wide arc of the rod to present an open loop thus keeping the weighted nymphs away from the rod and the back of your head!. In the casting action if you get it wrong and one of the nymphs crashes into the rod blank, it can damage it to the point that it will weaken and eventually snap. Having cast upstream and at an angle out to the desired area the nymphs are allowed to sink before an upstream mend is put into the line, leaving the end of the fly line in a tight 'u' shape curve above the nymphs drifting downstream on the current, another mend is put in as they go past your position and feed of loose line from the hand. The downstream current will pull this through gently and allow the nymphs to pass and fish a greater length of river at the right depth, the eyes are keyed in onto the 'u' curve / fold in the fly line on the surface to detect the takes. The tightening or strike again is a downstream 'towards your bank' motion to keep the flies in the area of the basement and middle floor. If you are mistaken on the faltering of the line, if you strike upwards then the flies are pulled up out of the area where they are more likely to be successful, whereas in the method I describe you will just pull them sharply along in the right area and this can sometimes induce a take. There is a trend these days to use a strike indicator, I have used them, but prefer the method I describe with the created fold in the line. Also the sight indicator style is not allowed in river national and international matches.

Another style with the 'bugs' that can be effective, when you are in and amongst a shoal of grayling on a fine gravely piece of the river bed, is to allow the point nymph to catch up on the bottom and drop the rod tip downstream so that the point of the rod is almost touching the water, with the line tight and in a straight line onto the point nymph. This allows the two droppers to fall onto the gravel below in the current, where you should let them rest for a few seconds, giving the rod tip a couple of quick upward twitches, only about an inch or so, creating a slight movement in the droppers off the gravel. Often the takes to this are fierce and positive, similar to those mentioned earlier whilst using a similar method with sea trout taught me by my father very many years ago - the only difference being that it was a downstream hang of the flies from the rod tip, whereas this method the rod tip is downstream of the nymphs.

The Mini lure method of approach can be used in any kind of water, but is best suited to a fast flowing current. The lure needs to pass close by the lie of the fish so the line is a fast sinker, the faster the better. It is cast across and slightly upstream to start with at the head of the pool and as soon as the cast is made the rod tip is placed in the river close to the river bed and the lure stripped back quickly with long pulls to ensure that the lure is fishing at the right depth. To tighten into a take, simply tug the line back in the retrieving hand to sink the hook point before you lift the rod out of the water. Subsequent casts are made in a fan like fashion from the point you are standing at, covering the likely lies through the entire pool. Casts are also made directly downstream and pulled back quickly along the sides, through any deep channel where fish could be holed up. It's a sure fire way of catching trout that have become cannibals too and, to be sure they are better out of any river system, a flash back to the quill minnow days on the River Wen, not many miles apart the only difference being in the presentation aspect, one with a fixed spool reel and a short stiff spinning rod, the other with a fly rod.

Of all the possible combination of methods and approach, these described have been my most successful, I have tried them all, you can be sure of that.

The Sea Trout

There is no other game fish known to have kept grown men away from their beds for so long and so often and for so many years as the magical, mysterious, sea going brown trout. The 'Sea trout' is a special fish and has a special place in my heart. If I were to be asked whether I preferred fishing for 'Salmon' or 'Sea trout', to be fair there's only one answer that I could come up with and that is to say 'both' of course. There is a definite art in successful fishing for both and whilst the Salmon can get you out of bed early in the morning, the Sea trout can keep you away from it all night.

A 'Brown trout' decides for reasons only known within its genes, 'I'm going out there into the salt to see what's there, especially hopefully - food', and off it goes, It finds rich pickings and that's enough for it to make its mind up that it will spend part of its life there and part in the river - teasing us with its secretive presence and all of the sudden frightening us with its leap and splash on the darkest of nights. As I write this the snow is falling heavily, and I can't wait for the time to come round again that I will be in its company, seeking it out with various tyings from the winter stock build up.

Yes the Sea trout is a great sporting fish and really a brown trout through and through - the difference is in the brain and the genes, one stays put in the river and the other goes to sea. Its distant cousin the Salmon is distinctly different, not only in its make up but in appearance also, whilst both are silver when they return to the river, there are four positive identifying features that are recognisable.

If you lie a salmon and sea trout alongside each other and look for the following, you will see the differences immediately and once seen never forgotten. The first point is the length of the maxillary bone above the mouth - in a salmon the bone's length will be level with an imaginary line drawn vertically at the back of its eye, in the sea trout the bone will extend beyond this imaginary line. The second point to look for is the lateral line running the whole length of the fish - in salmon, there will be no spots below this line towards the belly of the fish, whereas in the sea trout there will be. Below and along the scale line at an angle between the adipose fin and the lateral line in a salmon you can expect eleven to thirteen scales, in a sea trout there will be over thirteen, the scales being smaller on a sea trout. The last thing you should look at is the tail - the salmon's will be slightly forked and slanting towards the body of the fish and the sea trout slightly square to protruding outwards between the tips. There is also the fact that the wrist in the salmon's tail is more solid on the outer edges running into the tail whereas in a sea trout it is not so pronounced. If you put all of these together you can identify one from the other. Mind you, having said that, there are hybrids now and again and these can be confusing.

Are Sea trout easier to catch than Salmon? That is a question worth attempting to answer. Let us look at a month during the high season June and July. Whilst opportunity will exist to catch both species I would argue that there are probably more conducive conditions to go in pursuit of the Sea trout than there are for Salmon. This is, due to weather patterns in the main. Whilst Sea trout will take an offering during the day and night, salmon seldom take at night. Although there are reported exceptions to this, in the main the Salmon is a daytime fish and the Sea trout a night time fish. I've always wondered on this point alone whether there is in fact a pecking order between the two species, when they are younger and that the Salmon Parr feed mainly in the daytime whereas the Seatrout Parr do so at night, we can never be sure.

In periods of 'good' water during the high season there is a likelihood that you can catch Sea trout in the daytime, whilst fishing for Salmon, especially so in spate rivers. We only have to look at the River Tweed for the results - whilst more

Salmon are caught, Sea trout are caught daily also in all heights of water.

Salmon tend to run upstream on high water and as the water is dropping off, and they will hold up until that water comes. The Sea trout however will not wait, and will push and scrape through not only in high water but in the lowest water conditions.

As detailed earlier when I wrote about the River Dwyfawr, I do regard myself very fortunate to have seen and experienced the times of plenty as far as this magical fish is concerned. I had also an added advantage in my earlier years of following in the footsteps of my father in their pursuit both day and night, employing various methods and techniques to succeed.

In a Sea trout season, you could expect some fish in late May although some rivers are earlier than this. It is mainly dependant on the call of the fresh water. If we have a flood in the river in late April, May, then the Sea trout will make an appearance, the larger fish coming in first. Great shoals of them will lie up in the pools in the lower reaches as they acclimatise prior to their journey upstream. A pool on a river can appear to be devoid of any presence or activity, but the hidey holes under trees alongside boulders and under banks can be full of fish which, at certain times of the day, will move around. Later in the year as the first-year run fish come in, they will shoal up and can easily be seen from any vantage point above a pool, given the right light conditions.

If the water in the river is high the fish will move upstream and spread out breaking up the shoals into smaller groups and individual fish. They will have their favourite places in the rivers and you have to seek these out. Remember that there is no substitute for experience on this front, certain lies in certain pools will be taking spots and this can vary at differing heights of water flow. You also have to seek these places out - remember the 'restaurant' and 'waiter', approach works in all kinds of angling and if you approach with this in mind you increase your chances of success.

For daytime fishing for these great fish, the best is a falling water after a flood There are area's that can not be successfully fished with a fly and at those times the worm and or the spinner can come into play. As the fish are constantly on the move in their upstream surge, you can chose to stay put in one pool that suits you or you can move quickly from pool to pool and cover a large area. Personally, I prefer to be on the move. I have found this to be more successful because I believe that not every pool fishes in the same manner in all heights of water. By moving you can be covering more taking lies rather than waiting for the fish to come into the pool you are at in the hope that the height of water in that pool will be just right when they arrive.

Night time fishing in high water is not as productive on fly as it is when the river starts to settle to a more normal flow pattern. Possibly the reason for this is that the fly is whisked through the taking area quickly and also the fish tend to be on the move. I'm not saying that you will not catch, especially so on dusk and for about half an hour after dark, but the taking period is soon over and time is better spent on such nights gaining those brownie points at home. All is not lost however as you can be tidying and replenishing the fly boxes.

One method that does work well in high water is the 'worm' at night but only at certain times of the year. I recall as a young boy in the company of my father in September in the upper reaches of the river Dwyfawr when he had a bag of four fish for 17lb in weight in one small pool in and amongst a torrent of flood water. The fish, moving upstream, stopped momentarily in small lee and there they took the worm. This would be followed by exceptional excitement as they took off downstream, cart wheeling as they went. It was not totally dark, it rarely is, as there was a full moon appearing periodically between the clouds. The same method was used for fishing the worm in the daytime and I recall that Dad had the end of the fly line painted up with white paint so that it assisted him to evaluate the depth the worm was fishing at, I've tried it myself, but with little success compared to my father's skills. The water has to be right, the time of year right, the temperature right and doing the right thing in the right place - not easy to get it together often.

So it was during my teenage years that I was schooled in the art of catching Sea trout at night on fly and as I have mentioned before, there were two flies in the main that were used for the purpose -a Mallard Blue and Silver and a Mallard and Claret, both on size 8 hooks. (Page 200) They were attached to an eight foot leader and a slow sinking line. At the beginning I used a silk line on a split cane, three piece, 12ft rod loaned to me by my father.

In my youth I never had cause to use any other fly pattern at night, the team above always worked.

Those early years were very exciting and the magic has stayed with me ever since, and in the way that my father helped me, I derive as much pleasure today in guiding someone to success in the art as I do catching them myself.

The lower reaches of the river Dwyfawr has a number of great holding pools that are easily accessible and relatively easy to fish. It's not a large river by any standards and only short casts are needed in the main. When the cast is made the whole lot is allowed to drift round on the current and no retrieve is introduced until the very end when the line is on the hang. Then the rod tip is moved upstream very, very slowly. I always angle the line off the tip of the rod as this prevents smash takes, the angle reducing this risk as the bend in the rod will cushion the suddenness and ferocity of sea trout takes.

With the modern lines of today, I use a floater with a braided sink tip leader which I fashion myself out of level clear nylon braid rubbed with a mixture of sink dough and varnish. I have these in lengths of 18" through to 48" with a loop at each end and can easily swap them to alter the depth at which the flies are presented to suit the needs both of the pool being fished and my own imagination of how they should swim through the lies in those pools. All trial and error techniques until you build up a mental memory of what works where and at what water height and in what conditions, not easy for a beginner. I also use intermediate lines right through to a Di 3 where necessary to get the business end down to the gravel bars where those silver beauties rest up. Naturally if you have a pool that is 15' deep and a good flow travelling through it you would have to go heavier in the sink rate of line for it to get down to the fish, for they will not move off their lie at times to take the offering.

My night would start when I could not see the green colour in the grass on the bank. Another sign is that the bats appear, but do not be too eager for you could spoil the pool for yourself later. I find that the colour going out of the grass is a sure safe sign that the best time was approaching and sitting there quietly alongside the water I would notice a movement in the water surface now and again as the fish coming from their hidey holes jostled for positions on the shallow glides and at the tail of the pool. Sometimes fish could be seen entering the pool with a 'V' shape appearing. Such fish sometimes lie in the fast turbulent well oxygenated water below the pool and come into the quieter tail of the pool at night. Locating a shoal of fish during the day is one thing, knowing where they will lie up at night is another and it is through trial and error in the approach that this knowledge is derived. To my annoyance, I found more times than I care to remember that I have disturbed a fish from its lie at my feet through being too eager to cast over where the shoal had been lying up during the day. This can vary according to the height of the water running through the pool. There is, of course, no substitute for experience on particular rivers. You just have to go through the apprenticeship of learning the pools and knowing of the ways of the pool and the ways of the Sea trout in those pools at differing heights of water.

Angling the cast in and allowing the sweep of the line through lengthening the line after each cast in a fan like fashion taking a step after every other cast is the normal method adopted until the pool is fished out. Whilst doing this one notes mentally any particular spot that a tweak is felt or even a thump and you do get them sometimes, remarkably with no hook-up. I don't know how they do it? Anyway such spots are key taking areas and directional angles are registered in the mind's eye ranging from the feel of where your feet are, the depth the water vis a vis your waders, right through to bank side vegetation and position of trees. This is so that when you come through the pool next time, later on the same night you have a good idea where to place yourself and the angle at which to fish. Then through either upstream mends or even downstream mends you present the fly in a different fashion over the lie or a different fly even. More often that not it secures a solid take and contact with the Sea trout and you will not have been quite so surprised by the take. It is definitely a thinking game and the Sea trout are in charge at all times, never kid yourself otherwise.

For much of my fishing life I used standard size 8 flies to start with in normal summer flows for night fishing whereas if on the latter end of a dropping water I would use size 8 long shank and in heavier water a 6 long shank. Again the same patterns, Mallard Blue and Silver and Mallard and Claret, I rarely needed anything else. As the night progresses I changed the flies to the long shank 8 and on to size 6 to suit.

These days I also favour an aluminium tube for the point 1" to 2" to 3" depending on the flow and a size 6 or 8 long shank Dovey Black and Orange on the dropper, but that is in the River Dee, Dovey or Conway, larger rivers, where most of my Sea trout fishing now takes place. The reason for this is due to a heavier flow of water through the pools - the heavier flies seem to fish through the lies better. I also use a wake lure and a secret weapon which is based on the Mallard Blue and Silver, on a size 6 long shank hook. For the dressing of the 'Secret weapon' a fly that has often saved the night from being fishless, I set the treble an inch away from the hook bend on stiff nylon which is level with the end of the wing. The fly is fished on the point of a team of two in the normal fashion - there's something about the way that it swims that attract the fish and of course the flying trebles do catch the tail nippers. (Page 199 / 202).

I seldom fish before midnight now , I find that the better fish take later in the night. An aside here is that at around 1am to 2am especially so in July I catch quite a number of Grayling on the Tube fly, fish in the 2 .5 to 3lb in weight. You think you're in to a good sea trout because they jump when you hook them and then very quickly just give in. I try not to fish too long a line if I can help it, just enough so that I do not frighten the fish in my approach.

Weather patterns are also very important and have an impact on whether you have good or bad nights for Sea trout fishing. A clear night with the air temperature falling and dropping below the water temperature is not good normally as a mist will form and rise off the river – known as 'tarth' in Welsh. The first sign of this happening is when you run your hand along the rod blank and you find it is wet. In the height of summer with the mist forming and the water temperature high, don't be too eager to depart the river because later on if the mist rises, its effect on the water temperature will have been good, dropping it down a few degrees and the fish then come on to the take. A heavy, hot, clammy kind of night with thunder rumbling in the distance, is not good usually either although it does not mean that you will not catch fish at all. It just means that it will be more difficult as the atmospheric pressure is dropping either rapidly or steadily away and it seems to put the fish right off. The best kind of night is with a soft breeze and a few drops of rain now and again, and very dark - the Sea trout become very active in this kind of weather and the takes seem to be more positive than on other kind of nights. I have also caught Sea trout when the rain has been falling steadily especially so after a long period of drought. On this kind of night, the barometric pressure will have steadied off and when the rain arrives the river livens up.

My father showed me a very useful method employed in extracting Sea trout from the tail section of the 'Concrete' pool on the Dwyfawr in no more than eighteen inches of water. I had a level silk line possibly a number two, which equates to about a five or six weight AFTM. The length of line cast was possibly no more than about five yards out of the tip of the rod. The armoury at the business end was a size eight Mallard Blue and Silver on the point and a Mallard and Claret on the dropper, three inches long half way down a cast of eight feet in length. I would cast out to mid river, across and down fashion and allow the cast to work round without a retrieve. Initially the fish would take on the sweep across and after a while they would go off this kind of presentation. The rod tip would follow the line downstream and in towards my bank.

The next method adopted would be to cast in the same fashion and introduce a slow figure of eight retrieve about half way through the cast, this would bring a few more takes until the fish wised up. With these methods the flies were pulled through and above the shoal of fish at the tail of the pool. When all went slack again another method was brought into play - same cast, same follow down and across leaving the rod tip at a slight angle to the line, out towards the middle of the river. No retrieve was imparted and the whole lot allowed to sink onto the gravel and left there, the rod tip would then be moved ever so slowly upstream and I mean really, really slow, and steady, the flies would only move an inch or so and bang! The fish would hammer into the flies, this was possibly the most devastating of the methods at this location. However, as fishing goes sometimes none of the methods would work, but a single maggot on the point fly would take the odd fish, even a miniature worm half an inch long attached to the fly will induce a take. It's well worth bearing these points in mind for you never know when they will come in useful.

As time moved on with improvement in tackle and experiences encountered, skills became finer tuned but even so, there is only one sure thing in angling and that is the unexpected. The skilled angler will overcome each obstacle placed before him and more often than not succeed in his quest compared with the less experienced who will struggle to achieve.

I can not emphasise enough the value of mending the line either to hold or quicken the flies through a chosen lie. An upstream and across mend holds the flies on the lie for longer whilst the downstream mend quickens and drags the fly through. If you want your fly to sink further, cast it four or five feet above the lie and kill the cast in mid air before it lands, you are not looking here for a perfect turnover, in fact you are looking to dump it. Feed the slack through the rings and allow the fly to dead drift into the lie. It will sink as it travels downstream, deeper than any other cast without changing the line, put a stop to everything and as it tightens up in the current above and in the lie there is some sudden movement in the fly caused by the stop in the rod and the effect of the current on the line, just as if it has come to life. Prepare yourself for a reaction from the fish.

I never present the flies constantly in the same fashion over the same lie, never more than twice before I move my feet and search out another area. This has served me well for nearly half a century.

Oh how I wish for a return to those early days and times of plenty, if it were just for those of you who did not experience it so that you could see the vast shoals that existed then. I hear it said and often spoken of today, 'The pool is full of fish' and I get excited and go and have a look only to find a small shoal of up to twenty or so fish hanging on the current near to the tail of the pool. It was literally hundreds in layers in days gone by, the colour of the river would change as the fish moved about and I've only experienced that once in the last twenty years and that was shoals of 'Bonefish' off one of the Islands in Great Exuma being herded about by some Barracuda. It was just like sheepdogs herding a flock of sheep, the colour in the sea changed as they moved about.

I recall an Otter coming into a pool on the Dwyfawr and the fish panicking and the pool surface boiling with the disturbance and fish swimming out onto the gravel banks and flopping about before falling back in. It was an amazing sight but that was then and this is now and we have to live with what life throws at us and make the most of it. Who knows what will happen next, it may well be cycles that we go through and it is actually on the cards to return. Although I may not be around to see that I sincerely hope it happens.

The 'Surface Lure' (Page 202) is a tool never to be overlooked in the quest for a 'Sea trout' - the darker the night the better. It is also used for seeking out the location of lies in a pool. I'll explain. You have fished the flies through the pool with no success, trying the variety of differing presentation methods described and still nothing. Then you put on a surface lure and immediately you get a reaction. Now I'm not saying a 'strike' at the lure but a reaction from the fish, bulges around the lure and boils at it. This shows you that they are there. On many an occasion I have happened upon a pool where an angler present has commented that there were no fish in the pool after which I put a surface lure which bore no hooks on and proceeded to show its use to an often amazed onlooker.

The use of the lure is enhanced in presentation styles again through the use of upstream / across / and downstream mends, sometimes following on to each other in the same cast to give a tight bend in the line above a suspected lie. Sometimes the fish will not hesitate and will crash into the lure, other times they will tweak at it and often just boil around it - very exciting fishing.

I sometimes fish the surface lure on a short dropper with a size 6 long shank fly trailing 2 feet behind, the fish swirl around the surface lure and on their return to the lie will often take the trailing fly, very fiercely.

I also move around on the pool casting at different angles, it often brings a response from the fish. On many an occassion I have successfully used the surface lure to catch Brown trout which are either 'Cannibals' or becoming such - fish of 1lb to 2lb in weight with large mouths and slender bodies, usually carrying remnants of fish in their stomachs. They are a bonus and are well rid of from rivers as they do untold damage to fish stocks if allowed to live on. I boil these and feed them to the dogs at home, they love their treat.

The Atlantic Salmon

The king of fish will have his way, always. Take comfort from the fact that when you do succeed, they have only let you in momentarily for they will switch that light off when they are good and ready and that will happen as suddenly as they switched it on. What I aim for here is to prepare you or enhance your capabilities or even share with you some experiences based upon my observations of the complex issues that are involved.

You will recall that I have previously mentioned certain conditions during which I have been successful in catching fish or have witnessed that success. I have taken myself back to those early years in childhood and youth to identify some of that guidance which has helped frame my approach to all my fishing especially so Salmon fishing today.

I was fortunate in that my father in his approach spoke to me about what he did in fishing. Possibly some of this was due to my persistent presence at every move when he was into his fishing tackle especially if there was an outing on the cards. Not only did he describe in detail where he did it and when but he also proved it over and over again and repeated and enhanced upon his own experience and my knowledge of those experiences and times of success. Of course, just like everyone else, we also experienced very many blank sessions, but on reflection, I can not seem to recollect many reasons as to why those failures arose. Possibly the memory does not attach itself to the detail of such happenings but only does so when success is experienced - maybe something in the brain comes in to shade over failure. You do not forget it but it's not quite so vivid and clear as the gilt framed success stories. Perhaps all life is a bit like that?

I recall in my early teens coming home from school on the bus and as we came over the bridge of the river Erch I registered a full-blown brown flood. By the time I was in Chwilog, two miles later, my mind was in the inquisitive mode and, as I walked the few hundred yards from the bus to my home, my step quickened as I realised in my own mind that there were rolling cotton wool clouds and there was a warm wind. My step developed into a gallop which was met at the back door by my father who told me to get ready if I wanted to go with him, thus it was a major quick disposal of the school uniform into every corner of the bedroom and prior to the sound of the final stroke of the nine day clock in the hallway, I was at a jam sandwich and scone prepared by my mother and ready for the off.

What had been instilled into me in those early years was the type of weather conditions that would be suitable for a visit to the upper Dwyfor where there would be a chance of success. This of course was coupled with the height of water, time of the year and time of the day. My memory does not recall that particular day further than that, but, suffice to say that such days became the grounding upon which today I base decisions of shall I go or shan't I.

Sarah, my wife, has witnessed many an occasion when, in the middle of doing something totally unrelated to fishing around the home, I have dropped all tools as it were, and I've gone to the river Dee only to return within an hour or so with a Salmon. I can not describe it accurately for you, neither can I tell you what it is, but, something happens atmospherically which I relate to. It triggers my mind into realising that the conditions are just right and I don't let that chance slip away. In fact I don't spend as much time now actually fishing at all times but rather I watch and wait for the right moment to practice the art in. You can also adapt to this kind of approach based on experience and registering in the mind the conditions when you catch each fish. Pick up on this and store it for the future for there will be a moment, a time, during most days that will afford you a better chance of success. I have had a fish in the morning and then gone off to do something else for the rest of the day only to return sometimes hurriedly to catch another later on the same day. These days I ask everyone I see with a fish to give me details of the time of capture and I fit that information into a loose pattern which I base my approach on time wise. It's not bullet proof but a great guide within the mind and a continual mental picture of what is occurring from day to day and week to week and realistically from river to river as the season progresses.

What an incredible fish the Salmon is, to evolve from its gravel based nest (red) as a fertilized ova through the hatching and aelvin stage into a fry - developing the gills and feeding on the tiniest aquatic organisms which carry the protein needed for its growth. Then, on through the Parr stage with its voracious feeding habit of any morsel present and on to smolting and the migration downstream from the upper reaches over various obstacles to the sea. It then goes through the stages of osmosis into the salt on its outwards journey to far away seas without compass, map or any other device known to man. Miraculously it returns as a grilse or adult salmon overcoming all the obstacles of predation and man made pollutants of all kinds to once again go through the biological imbalance of osmosis on return to fresh water. Finally, the upstream migration to reach the spawning beds providing us, on the way, with a sport fit for kings. Its brain in dissection is only the size of a pinhead in a fry and a pea in an adult fish and I wonder if its map is the position of the stars coupled with its sense of smell for the minor roadways in its mind? Wonder and sheer magic. Let us look at 'Salmon on a Fly' possibly the most thrilling of all the methods especially so if you have dressed your own. If you've never had a casting lesson with a double handed or even a single handed rod, I urge you to do so with a certificated qualified Instructor. It will enhance your fishing beyond belief, it did me, 'but I'd rather spend the money on fishing', well more fool you.

I like to fish for Salmon with a double handed rod because of the presentation aspect. I need to hang that fly over the lie long enough to entice its occupant to get annoyed with it and take it into its mouth to remove it from its vision. Sometimes of course the delivery of the cast and its presentation over the lie needs to change, and a single handed rod is better suited for that form of presentation - more on that later. The pull is felt on the line and the fly hook pulled back sufficient to sink the point, that's what it takes, no more no less. Look upon the basics and keep it simple, keep moving your feet and altering the angle of the presentation. It really is the best advice any angler can take with him in the pursuit of the Salmon. Also go back to where I earlier described each pool in the 'Approach and the Methods', as a restaurant which, with varying water heights, will have those Salmon sitting at different tables. On a particular lie in a particular height of water you may have some indication that there is a fish in that lie - do you just cover it with a cast from one angle? No, watch the current in the upper layers and watch what happens and how your fly swims through it. Angle the cast in differently or move your feet to another location so that the cast fishes out in a different manner over the chosen spot - it will pay dividends eventually.

Another consideration is that should a fish show interest in a fly and refuse it, change the fly, same pattern but go down in size and try again - the results are almost always the same, the fish is enticed again and takes the fly provided it has not moved. I recall doing this on the river one day, working downstream, the fish showed three times on the fly even when I went down in size, in high water conditions and then disappeared. I quickly moved back upstream into the next pool and covered a known lie, eight casts and then up he came and took it. Now I can not be certain that it was the same fish, but there is a likelihood that it was, as I had seen it a few minutes before. In support of the claim I have a DVD available entitled 'Salmon on Fly' where a Salmon came to the fly twice and refused it. A quick change to a smaller fly of the same pattern and it took on the very next cast. On the same DVD I show that when fish were moving in one pool on high water and showing no interest in the fly, by moving upstream just above some rapids onto another taking lie I had another. Those moving fish stop momentarily on their upstream surge and if you can cover them then, they will show interest. It is only through experience of this that I know it works and you can develop your own skills to suit. The list is endless and that is the magic of 'fishing' with rod and line, for you never really know what is going to happen next – especially with salmon.

Another point to illustrate the importance of presentation., but on a beat I intimately knew in the upper Welsh Dee I was guiding on one occasion with one angler in the morning and another in the afternoon. One had never fished for salmon before and the other had never caught a salmon. I recall arriving on the beat, the water level was perfect. The first angler was taught the basics of roll casting and by lunchtime, with me standing against his shoulder, he had banked two Salmon, and dropped another. I repeated this with the other angler in the afternoon and he also had two whilst other accomplished salmon anglers also present on the same beat caught nothing! Why should this be so? Luck you may say - and that may be so, but, based on the numbers of fish banked, it was probably more to do with the way the fly was presented over the taking lies, the correct angle to optimise the chances of success. That comes with experience. However good one is, and I include myself in this, it pays to analyse situations and put into practice good and varying fly presentations in order to succeed.

Another occasion on the same beat, I arrived at lunchtime and met two anglers that had been there all morning and caught nothing. The water was slightly up off summer level and also slightly coloured. One of the anglers had seen fish but had not made any contact.

There is a shallow gravely run just above the fishing hut known as the 'Run out of Charlie's' which had not been tried, the water was slow moving but steady all the way across. I had lunch with them and put up a 9 feet, seven weight, single hander, floating line with a five foot long, fast sinking braided leader – in fact it was the Sea trout kit in the car from the night before. Onto this I tied a 9 foot leader of 10 lb. breaking strain and attached to it two flies, a Black and Silver size 10 treble on the point and a Peter Ross another size 10 single, on the dropper.

I approached the pool about half way down and laid a cast across directly to the other bank, throwing into the cast a downstream mend and another after it had landed from the loose line in my hand. I allowed a few seconds for it to sink, put the rod tip down to the river pointing it across to where the cast had initially been laid and used a fast figure of eight retrieve. The line coming back in a down stream arc, stopped half way across and I lifted into a lively grilse of three and a half pounds. One of the anglers netted it for me. He could not believe it. I rested the area for a few minutes and cast again to show him the method and repeated the presentation that had banked the grilse. On that very next cast I had a Sea trout of just over four pounds. Now it doesn't always work, but in the main with such a small rise of water it can be very good provided it is practiced in the right place and at the right time.

On another occasion again I went to the same beat to find two angling friends present and fishing on a high but clearing water. Neither had caught fish although one of them had bent the rod into one, but it had parted company with the fly almost as quickly. I asked the question of them if they had been over to the far bank to fish a pool called 'Charlies' which was un-fishable off the bank we were on due to the height of water - neither had.. I suggested that one of them went to do that, but they declined, so with their approval I drove the car round a two-mile run to get to the other bank. In an hour I took four Salmon on the fly which I duly returned to the river, whilst they remained blank for the day. The crucial factor here was that I read the water and the conditions in a different way to which they had, that gave me advantage over the situation. I moved position and it was rewarded.

There is no secret, it is reading the water and making the right decision to suit the conditions and, more importantly, angling the cast correctly to cover the lie - making that fly irresistible. You may recall reading earlier of one of my first escapades to the upper Dwyfor as a child with my father when he said to me after a head and tail rise to the fly in high water when the fish refused the offering, **'I was stood in the wrong place'** where upon he moved his feet and caught it on the next cast. That lesson has proved its usefulness to me hundreds of times over the years. The best advice I can give you, is to keep moving your feet to get the angle right, then remember exactly where you were stood when a fish took you on every pool where it happened . It will repeat itself over and over given similar con ditions, or until the actual lie changes with the changing river bed after high water, then you have to search it out again.

At the same time, you also have to consider the length and type of line you are making the presentation with coupled with the fly you are presenting. In essence if you are casting down and across the stream at a 45 % angle on a shortish line the fly will come through the lie fairly quickly, whilst a tighter angle on an even shorter line would take it to 75% quickening the travel of the fly through the lie. With a longer line from further upstream the cast is angled differently, shallower maybe 25% and that will slow down its travel through the lie.

In addition to this you can control the speed by throwing mends either upstream or downstream to get the fly to act in a different manner. Aerial mends and mends on the water should always be thrown from slack line in the hand and not directly off the tip of the rod as this will enable the fly to continue to sink or swim more naturally through the lie.

As to lines, these days I use a Floating Spey style line with a head length of 65feet, with 5ft and 10ft sinking leaders to suit - usually medium to fast sinking for most of my fishing with a single fly. This can alter through to very fast sinking heads up to 25ft long which are attached to a shooting head backing. I find them easy to control on a double handed rod. This set-up gives me the flexibility to tackle any water conditions that I am likely to encounter.

If fishing a spate river I like to use two flies on the cast, especially so if there are sea trout present. It gives me the option to present the flies in various ways as I move along from pool to pool. I will walk sometimes two miles in a session, searching out eddies and glides and dangle the dropper fly alongside fast currents into what I term holes that fish rest up in on their upstream runs. When I come on to a pool I vary the angles of the cast in an across and down method. Finally, I seldom use a single handed rod in a spate where the banks are tree strewn and the river bed boulder strewn because the length in a double handed rod has distinct advantages in presentation terms when fishing such waters. If the banks are clear and the pools large then the single handed rod comes into its own.

I recall one fine day's fishing on the Dwyfawr. It was in early August 1978 and the river was in flood and fining off on my arrival. I walked down from Cefn Uchaf footbridge to a footbridge below the Widow's Pool, an area I knew well and had visited on numerous occasions since my childhood. I fished all the way back up on the Ty Cerrig side ending up with a bag which consisted of four fish - a 13lb Salmon and three Sea trout of 3lb, 5lb and 6lb all taken on a Corff Melyn Budyr (Dirty Yellow Body) and a Coch-y-Bonddu on the dropper size 6. (Page 204) I fished all the eddies and pools but the fish came from small glides alongside turf banks right up against the side. I saw every take in the clearing water, which was really exciting.

The Salmon came first and in such a location that it was impossible to follow its downstream run in between large boulders. It was a small hole type glide which I fished with two yards of fly line off the tip of the rod thereby giving the flies movement by imparting a small bounce to the tip of the rod. I was stuck on the bank in between two trees and had to poke the rod out over the river to hold the line out away from a willow that was growing half in the river, half on the bank. The fish went out to the far bank and downstream in the fast current past a boulder half the size of a car which was just covered in streaming and boiling water. Fortunately, I was able to lift the line back over the rock as the fish darted downstream taking all the fly line and some twenty yards of backing. by the time it stopped. Initially, it had gone round the small pool several times and I'd just managed to hold it there on 15lb leader. I had seen Salmon do this before and watched what my father had done

149

more than once. I waited for a number of minutes and could just about make out a slight kick by the fish on the rod every now and then - it could have been the water pressure, I was not sure.

It was totally unsafe and unsuitable to wade as I could have never held my feet in the fast water. Anyway after what appeared to be quarter of an hour of this I took some more backing off the reel and wound this by hand around the fly reel to lock it, it was in the days before clutches were the norm on fly reels, before pulling the rod back and placing it well back in the marsh. I quickly walked downstream counting the paces as best I could to give me some guide as to where the fish could be, when I came to a pool that we knew as 'Llyn Niel'. There was an elderly gentleman ledgering a worm there, sat on a small stool, I believe he was a visitor by his accent and the style of fishing he had adopted. I asked him if he had seen a fish splash about and he confirmed that he had and pointed downstream towards the tail end of the pool, I excused myself and explained that my rod was upstream and that it was on my line. He looked at me in amazement when I got my gaff out and dipped it into the river in front of him. I knew that the water pressure would wash the line to my side of the river and I managed to trap the line on the bend of the gaff, lifted it out and grabbed hold of it. I gently hand lined the Salmon to the side further downstream and slipped the gaff into its gill and out he came. It is illegal to be in possession of and use a gaff these days. After the last rites were administered I took the cast off and dropped the line back in the river, went back upstream, picked my rod up and wound the line back in, re connected the fly leader and off I went downstream, bidding the elderly gentleman good day and good luck.

I recall every location that I took fish from that day especially as each of the sea trout made acrobatic encounters of their respective takes to the dibbled coch-y-bonddu on the dropper. Only one further problem arose, the point fly got caught up in some moss on a rock out in the river with the sea trout on the dropper in between. Again it was drop the rod, hand line right down to the cast and a lift of the sea trout out by putting my finger in its gill and pulling it free, moss and all.

On my way back up the river on the opposite bank, having walked round the lower bridge (Pont ffatri) I came to the pool where I had seen the visiting gentleman fishing. He was just packing up and showed me a lovely Seatrout of about 4lb he had caught on the worm, I was very pleased for him.

It was some weight of fish in total that I carried back that last half mile to the car and by this time the sun had broken through and was bright and above me. By the time I got back I was lathered in sweat. Then back for a quick lunch with my mother before my journey back to Wrexham. What an outing - I lost another three fish that day without seeing them clearly. I sometimes use this method on the River Dee too alongside fast runs but it is not as effective as it is on a spate river.

I recall another occasion in the same location when the journey round the two bridges resulted in eight fish hooked and lost - the fish coming short to the fly on each occasion. There was nothing that I could have done that would have changed it as there was little or no cloud cover. It is important to register these changes in weather and marry them up with success and failure - for you will happen upon it in both directions often.

The latest method that I have learnt is the use of the fast sunk line in heavy water which is clearing and even coloured in a flood. The presentation is down and across at a 45% angle. Drop the rod tip almost to the river and jig the whole affair by pulling the rod hand back in 12" pulls and releasing back as the fly works its way round. You do get caught up on the bottom often but the fish have a go when the fly is jigged in front of them in their lies. I use a lightweight tube fly for this 2" to 3" in length and carry a supply of small trebles with me as they get blunt on the stones and the gravel. It works better on glides with a gravelly bottom try and avoid boulder strewn area's.

The beauty of this method is that it widens your opportunity to fish with the fly rod even in a big brown flood with a proven chance of success. However as with all Angling excursions you can never be certain of success.

The other method is the blackhead worm or lobworm as some may wish them to be identified. Some of you may seethe at the thought, even loose sleep over it. I have heard words worse than 'ungentlemanly' used to describe those that revert to the method, but worry not, if the method is legal and the conditions suit, skill is required for success.

I keep my worms in dampened newspaper and Sphagnum Moss that I collect from the bog, this cleans and hardens the worms making them tougher. The tub I use I store in a hole I have dug in the garden covered over with a concrete slab to ensure that the temperature is similar to their natural environment.

Boat fishing Lakes and Reservoirs

It was in the early seventies that I recollect my first experience of boat fishing and that was with John Ifor Thomas from Anglesey, a great angler and very much a specialist when it came to fly patterns. It was John that used a mixture of coloured tinsels off the Christmas tree to make a copy of a hatching chironomid.

My outings with John Ifor on Llyn Alaw in the early 70's were an experience that will be with me until that final breath, Oh what great times those were, Llyn Alaw was created as a reservoir in a shallow marshy valley in Anglesey and was initially stocked with fingerling Brown and Rainbow Trout, which grew rapidly. Four pound Browns and Rainbows were normal with some very much bigger. Memories of lazy head and tail rises by shoals of fish in the dying ripple and light in the height of summer when you were covered in Caenis and Sedges are still vivid in my mind's eye.

Llyn Alaw needed that calm kind of weather to be at its best as a gale of wind soon churned the place up to a muddy mess. There was a phenomenal stock of fish in it and the fishing was beyond belief if you hit the right kind of day or evening. The main line to use was a floater set on a three fly cast fashioned out of eight pound nylon. You needed the strong leader and plenty of backing as you could be in three feet of water for a hundred yards in some areas, and these fish looked for the old ditches. Searing runs were experienced when they looked for some sanctuary when hooked and the old hedges which sported blackthorn bushes had their roots still present underwater. Today I would guess that the ditches have all filled in and the roots rotted away.

I learnt the art of setting the boat on the drift and was well advised that the boat drifting broadside would go stern first down wind tracking slightly across the wave. This meant that you should look at the wave pattern and direction and set the boat to end up in a particular bay or past a particular known taking spot from half a mile away. If the wind changed or died down, then the ploy would change also.

The kind of wind that John enjoyed fishing in was that warm wind from the South West with some dampness in the air, not too strong, but strong enough to create a quiet whistle in the protruding parts of the outboard engine whilst on the drift. Sport would become fast and furious on such days. There was often a sudden change in the evening to an oily calm leaving wind lanes here and there on the water surface that trapped the insects and made fishing visual to rising fish in and on the edges of the lanes. Tactics would sometimes change from pulled and dibbled wet flies to static dries. It was mostly surface work with either slow sinking or floating lines - there was none of this deep line fishing in them days. The trout were different too, being more aggressive to a pulled fly caressing the waves on the bob and spectacular takes were experienced.

Whilst looking at the technique of the pulled wet fly in a wave, there are several considerations to bear in mind not least to use the position and drift of the boat to full advantage. Let us look at the short lining techniques first.

Consider having positioned the boat in a nice steady breeze and in a small wave and sitting in the bow of the boat on a broadside drift, you are set up with a slow sinking or floating line for working in the first six inches of water down from the surface. You have a boat partner who is in the stern, it matters not whether you are right or left handed but if left handed you need to be careful with your casting so that you do not catch your boat partner, on the back or forward cast. In front of you, central between the bow and stern take an imaginary line ahead in the direction the boat is drifting, through a ninety degree angle to your right to the point of the bow, that area of water is your fishing area. The area over to the left of the imaginary line is your boat partner's water. Your area in front of you through the entire ninety-degree angle should be covered in a fan like fashion in the casting, never casting in the same place twice.

If you cast directly in front of your position and proceed to pull the flies back towards the boat, you are covering a small area. Imagine that the fish are moving up the wave in a straight line in a shoal, potentially you are only covering one of these fish, who might not be interested in your offering. Angle the cast within the ninety-degree area across the wave slightly and you could be covering a number of fish in the shoal thereby increasing your chances. Also you are able to pull the flies across the wave, especially when at the end of your cast, the rod is lifted up to dibble the top dropper in the wave prior to making another cast.

Casting in the correct manner from a drifting boat is another way to increase your chances. Many a time I have watched anglers cast a long line whilst there is a good breeze and wave. This requires two or three false casts to get the distance. This is not really necessary because firstly your boat is drifting towards the fish and you will come across them eventually. Also your fly line might put fish that are nearer to the boat down, they don't take the fly line, they take the flies. To make two or three false casts to get distance takes time, multiply that time by the amount of casts you can make in a day afloat and evaluate the actual time that the flies are fishing in the water.

Using a shorter line requires one false cast or a roll cast followed by a single overhead cast. It does not take up as much time as the long line method, the fly line is not as likely to put fish down when it is short and the time factor that your flies are out of the water by comparison to the two or three false casts method is much less when evaluated over the whole of the fishing day. It is just common sense that your chances are enhanced, the more time your flies spend in the water.

However, this method is for certain conditions only and is for surface fishing. If the wind is very light with only a small ripple, it may well be worth casting further as there are other issues that could evolve. The fish can become boat shy or the air temperature is lower than that of the water which can mean that the fish are inactive on or in the surface area. You may have to fish deeper for them and use a faster sinking line and that will require a longer cast to allow the line to sink before you retrieve the flies back towards the boat. It's never bullet proof and only time and experience will enable you to be confident that your chosen method is the correct one.

In that oily calm with a dying light, small nymphs, emerging flies and dries through to the largest sedge patterns will have their chance for an airing. These are times when fish are spotted in the surface layers and their feeding paths gently intercepted with your chosen morsel. It's a time for delicacy and accuracy in the delivery and of course the correct pattern of fly to imitate what the fish may have been feeding on.

These were the methods that I used for a number of years in the development of my boat angling techniques and of different styles of presenting the flies in a wave, sometimes four of them on a cast. Whilst I have explained about the cast angled across the wave, another method is to use an even shorter line as described in the chapter on my first international match - a method I picked up off Cliff Harvey and still to this day put to good use when the conditions suit.

I have caught fish on this method in Llyn Brenig Grafham, Rutland, Chew, Blagdon, Draycote, Pitsford, Corrib, Ennell, Mask, Carra, Conn Loch Leven, Loch Harray and very many other Lakes and Reservoirs. Indeed almost everywhere that I have fished, provided that the conditions are suitable. With this sytem, the fly line is used to cast the flies a short distance from the boat and it is then lifted off the water almost immediately to allow the wind to put a forward bow in the line a simple roll cast is all it takes to get it out and there is no retrieve just the rod tip moving. You can pull a fly quicker that way than you can by stripping back the line. No line on the water means less for the fish to see and in reality if you cast ten yards to the side and front of the boat with this method and pick up the rod tip to create that bow in the line, by the time that the next cast comes to play the flies have travelled through a ten yard wide section of water to the side of you with a chance of covering more fish coming up the wave. Also just one roll and you are fishing again. In the right conditions you will be fishing, over a whole day afloat, twice as long as anyone casting conventionally overhead with false casts in-between.

Dry fly fishing from a boat is best suited to the warmer months of the year and to conditions of weather that in the main are calmer than that chosen for the pulled wet fly. The set up is quite simple with a two fly cast of about 14 feet long, Flies should suit the time of year to coincide with the hatches that occur or are expected, including terrestrial patterns and copies. In your ninety-degree area in front of the boat on the drift, the flies are cast out in a fan fashion searching to cover a fish below or cast to individual fish that are rising, either in a breeze or in calmer conditions.

You should attempt to cover the path that the fish is travelling in an attempt to intercept and fool it into taking your artificial offering. When dry fly fishing, I seldom if ever leave my fly on the water for longer than ten seconds, it is enough time for a fish to come and take it. I use a fairly short line of 10 to 15 yards which can be lifted off and dropped down in one cast again.The takes can be fierce affairs in a small wave right through to a small dimple sip in calmer water. Takes to semi wet or emerger patterns seem to be more leisurely than those to terrestrial patterns that float high.

I like the double strength nylon for my dry fly cast and normally use seven pounds breaking strain which even in a flat calm does not cause fish to shy away from the flies, I seldom use more than two flies on a fourteen foot cast. They are set seven feet apart and with a nine foot AFTM 6 weight rod provide a well balanced set up for a decent turnover.

Nymph fishing from a boat is now very popular on Lakes and Reservoirs, out over deep water. The static nymph, 20feet down, off a floating line will take some beating on some days. The method is relatively new, only in its infancy so to speak, but it is an effective yet relaxing method to fish with. Imagine being out there on a blistering hot and still day, not a fin in sight. Never say to yourself that the fish are inactive, they surely will be, but deep down.

You need the same rod set up as for the dries and a fluorocarbon leader of 18' to 20' long, preferably eight pound breaking strain and simple nymphs tied on heavyweight hooks. The cast is set out with the nymphs, three of them four feet apart. Select an area of the Lake or Reservoir where you will get a nice slow drift in the boat, using a drogue if necessary to slow the drift right down. Areas of the lake with about 20ft depth where there are weeds on the lake bed is very good.

Cast out about 20 yards of line, and do nothing other than to hold the rod low, tip six inches from the water surface and pointing down the line. The secret is to keep a straight line, allow the nymphs to sink and as the boat drifts on to them execute a very slow figure of eight retrieve. You are aiming to keep the line taught without pulling the nymphs back towards you. Now as the nymphs sink down, the end of your floating line will follow but worry not about this. Just when your boat drifts on top of your nymphs, keep on the figure of eight retrieve and start lifting the nymphs up through the layers, that can induce a take, there is nothing more natural than a nymph rising from the depths and these takes at that stage in the play can be fierce. That is why it is advisable to use at least eight pound breaking strain fluorocarbon. Keep watching the loop of line that exists between the rod tip and the water and you will in the event of a take see the line pull away slowly. Tighten into it immediately. Seldom do I feel the take when watching the loop, but I have had takes when I have momentarily looked away and its tap, tap, tap and then pull away, just like you would experience if you were fishing with a worm.

Nymphing in this way is a deadly method and one you should become conversant with as it can save the day for you. I recall visiting Lough Corrib in the early stages of the development of this kind of fishing. I had seen that great angler Micky Bewick use the method on Corrib the previous April when you could have called it Costa-del-Corrib! The temperature was in the eighties fahrenheit and the Lough's surface was like a sheet of glass. Frank Reilly was boating - Frank is a seriously good competitive angler and has secured the Irish Masters and also the World cup on the Western Loughs in Ireland - so he knew the Lough well and took us into Ballynalti Bay just off Greenfield. It was 'Olive' time and I asked if he could take the boat over a depth of twenty feet or so. Frank knew nothing of this static nymph method then, and he took us to a certain spot in the nine hundred acre bay. The boat was static, no drift as such and it took two hours to go possibly a hundred yards. There was only a couple of boats that left Greenfield that morning as everyone hoped for some sign of cloud or a slight breeze

I set up with a team of three nymphs as described and went for it with casts being aimed in different angles from the boat A quarter of an hour passed, nothing. Then, tap, then nothing - , strange - could have been a perch, I left it there for what seemed to be an age, before I saw the line pull away ever so slowly. I tightened in to a three pound wild brownie that went absolutely ballistic on me. I continued with this method for another hour or so and ended up with three more trout for a total weight of just over 12lb. What a cracking bag of fish and those Corrib trout are special to eat too!. It was enough fish for that week's visit and I took the cast off and gave it to Frank, who had watched the method with great interest and enthusiasm. (Plate 2 Page 104).

We met up with the other boats for lunch and I said nothing of the achievement of the morning's fishing and had agreed that Frank would not to say anything either. Questions were asked by the other boatmen - Mike Keady and Tom Doc Sullivan who all reported blanks. When I said that I had a bag of fish, they would not believe me and questioned my honesty with a few choice words. Frank eventually asked them to take a look under the wet sack in the boat and I enjoyed seeing the look on their faces! So you see, there are methods that work even in the most hopeless of conditions.

Having said that one must not stick rigidly to one method. The wind picked up on Corrib after lunch and the clouds started to roll in from the Atlantic, the 'Olives' hatched in droves and the fish moved on them for an hour or so. I changed to pulling wet dabbler size 14 in Olive. It worked well - all the fish caught were returned for the remainder of the weeks visit.

The method of sunk nymph fishing off a floating line is widely practiced on Corrib today and some phenomenal bags of fish are caught. I am pleased to say that most of the boatmen on Corrib now return their fish, only keeping one or two for the pot. Such is the case in many of the English and Welsh Reservoirs - for the stocked rainbows too so that they can grow on naturally, fins and all, and are thus much more pleasing to view and because they have become more naturalised on the food from the Lake or Reservoir.

The River Flies

Methods alone will not work unless you are confident with the business end of the set-up, the actual 'flies'. You will fish better and be more successful with a fly that you have confidence in than you ever will with a fly that you have no confidence in. I will not begin to go into detail about what is already written by many authors in the various books available, I will merely stick to what has been and still is very effective for me. I have records of my catches dating back to 1968 including details of flies used.

For the 'Dry' approach I use variants of established patterns, some with the addition of 'what I fancy' incorporated into the dressing, they are not the true original patterns as described elsewhere but are based on those patterns. Why rename someone else's developments when in fact it is a variant? Here are a selection of those I have found to work well season through:

The variant **'Sun fly'** in sizes 12 to 18. (Page 177).

The 'Sun fly' is a general pattern that represents a hoard of natural aquatic insects that hatch throughout the season and is made of the fur from a natural hare's mask from the actual ear. This is plucked out not cut. It is mixed well, placed within a dubbing loop for the larger pattern, spun and wound on. For the smaller version the fur from a natural rabbit's ear is again plucked and placed into a loop created by splitting the tying thread with the dubbing needle and spinning the bobbin holder creating a fine rope to wind on. The hackle in both cases is Cree or dark Coch y Bonddu. For my very smallest of the dubbed fur patterns I use mouse fur. As a general high floating pattern I've yet to find any fly that is worthy of a place alongside it in the fly box. We shall always be indebted to 'Dai Lewis' for creating it.

As a variant of this pattern I include a few turns of 'pearly' tinsel in the thorax area.

This variant of mine is tied using a Para loop fashion hackle sitting on top of the hook shank to allow the fly to fish in the surface film. This method of hackling is described in Ian Moutter's book, 'Tying the Paraloop Way'

The fully dressed larger pattern is fished in the rougher, riffley water at the head of a pool where it needs to float high. The smaller version and variants are fished through the glides. I use them from April right through to November.

'Sedges' an Emerger pattern. (Page 178)

Sedges play a large part in the diet of trout and grayling and from the second week in April right though to October these can be encountered on the river. I believe that there are 198 varieties of 'Sedge' in the United Kingdom of varying sizes and colour. Our first to hatch is the 'Grannom' which brings with it the first great rise of trout to 'Sedges' in any river around the second week in April depending on the temperature. The 'Sun fly' and its variants aptly copy the emerging and hatching insect on the surface film but I have another pattern of sedge emerger tied in mixture of 'F' fly and 'Parachute' fashion, on size 12 curved shank hook. The body is of spun fine SLF hair in three colours, light yellow at the tail, shading through a medium yellow to an orange in the thorax region. The natural cdc feathers are centred on the apex of the bend of the hook and set so as to point straight up with five or six needed to support the weight of a size 12 hook. To finish off I use a piece of black nylon tied in figure of eight at the head across the body and burnt to shorten and enlarge - copying the eyes of the natural. This fly has proved its worth on many occasions since it was developed in Lapland where I had struggled in a hatch of sedges - it is better in peaty stained water than in clear.

162

Some patterns to use when the **'Iron Blue Dun'** is hatching. (Page 178 / 179).

Around the same time in April and right through the season you may encounter a hatch of a small upwing fly, the Iron Blue Dun, always the case in broken showery weather. This also receives the attention of the trout and the grayling. A standard upwing pattern, a tail of a few strands of ginger cock hackle followed by a body created of a single strand of natural heron herl tied over a dab of superglue on the hook shank to strengthen the body. Starling secondary feathers are paired as wings, sitting short and upward from the hook shank, over wound fore and aft with a short fibered ginger cock hackle. This is an incredible simple pattern, but very effective and one I would not be without in size 14 and 16. I also tie a pattern to represent the Iron Blue Dun in 'F' fly fashion. Cul de Canard feathers for the wing. The tip of the body at the tail end is of claret tying thread or red prismatic tinsel, about 1/16" followed by the heron herl through to the thorax area. Deer hair tips on the 'F' fly version laid over the back of the hook shank below the cdc wing. These patterns are on curved shank hooks in size 14,16,18. I also have each of these patterns sporting a dubbed natural mole fur body, dressed very sparse. On their day they will out fish one another and also at certain times of the day this can happen, so rapid changes are required when the rise is on. I have no problem with this because I believe it is the way that it captures the light in the surface film and of course I have a supply of all the variants in the various sizes.

Some patterns to use when the **'Olives'** are hatching (Page 180 /181) Olives play a major part also throughout the season and in addition to the 'Sunfly' variant that I use, I also have great faith in the 'F' fly, 'Shuttlecock' and 'Parachute' olive coloured flies. It was the 'F Ffly' (Cul-de-Canon) that gave me that great day on the Tweed in 1998 described earlier and has since been first choice on the cast when searching for fish in any piece of water where there is no activity to be seen. This fly is now used by anglers all over the world and I have letters and e-mails from as far afield as New Zealand, the Czech Republic and Lapland where its use by various anglers has been very successful. To dress the Cul-de-Canon I tie them on a size 14 and 16 curved shank hook for the 'F' fly and 'Parachute', on 16 and 18 curved shank hooks for the 'Shuttlecock'. Full details are included on the dressing materials and style in the 'The Rivers International' chapter. I have recently enhanced on the Cul-de-Canon 'F' fly in that I now add a turn of fine pearly tinsel around the hook shank in the thorax area from underneath it looks like an air bubble

'Cul-de-Canon sight fly'. (Page 182)

The 'Dry' that I use for the New Zealand method with a lightweight nymph in front of the dry, the dressing is identical to the 'Cul-de-Canon' with the addition of a couple of dyed orange cdc feathers laid over the wing to enable easy sight detection - on a size 14 curved shank hook. The nylon from the hook bend to the nymphs does not seem to make any difference in the hooking properties of the 'Dry' and fish will engulf this at times.

'Nymphs for NZ style' don't be without the **'Rat'**. (Page 182)

As I am on the subject of the New Zealand method, the 'nymphs' used in front vary in size and in weight, from small tungsten beaded size 14 to size 18 on straight and curved shank hooks to leaded and lightweights of the same patterns. They are of varying colours from bright yellow to black, orange, pink, etc and for some reason on their day they will all catch fish. There is one particular pattern that is a favourite and I call it the **'Rat'**, although the body is created with mouse fur, **'Mouse'** sounds a bit on the timid side. for this little pearl has caught an incredible quantity of fish and is a simple pattern to tie, in sizes 14 and 16.

For the heavier nymphs and when using two in front of the 'dry' the sight fly needs to be larger and more buoyant a Klinkhammer type of fly is desireable. (Page 183)

Another nymph, which is of great importance with this method of approach and presentation, is the 'Pheasant tail nymph' in a size 14, this with ten turns of fine lead wire in the thorax area. (Page 183)

One never to be without when the river 'Chironomids' are hatching and laying their eggs. '**The Bulbous Gnat'** (Page 184)

There is one other fly for the River that I would never be with out, and that is a female chironomid copy. I was on the middle reaches of the river Dee in mid July and there was a major hatch of chironomids on a hot sultry type of day in mid after noon. There were millions on the water surface floating down and the trout and grayling were having a bonanza - in some areas you would swear that it was raining, such was the density of the rise. Try as I did with various patterns down to size 22 I could not contact any of them, truly frustrating. This troubled me initially so I got my landing net and pulled the net on it together and held it in the surface film to trap the insects going by, lifting it up every so often to examine the trapped aquatics. They were all hatched out and some were flying off, dip and wait, same again all small back chironomids. I think it was on the third dip that I noticed one of the chironomids had a very bulbous abdomen and realised that it was the female returning to the water to lay its eggs. Further detailed viewing on the water surface revealed that possibly one in every five hundred was a female and it was this particular fly that the grayling would take each time, from in and amongst dozens of males. Once I noticed one pass I would keep my eye on it and watch it down the pool and sure enough a neb would appear and the fly disappear.

Back home that evening I set about tying a parachute type chironomid with a bulbous abdomen. This was achieved through winding black tying thread over each other in figure of eight fashion on the curved shank of a size 18 hook. When this was done I tied off the tying thread and painted over the created abdomen with clear nail varnish and allowed it to dry. The pattern was finished off by using a grey coloured antron yarn post and a tiny black hackle with the feather barbules length suited to the hook size. Next day I was back in the same location and sure enough mid afternoon the same happened again, but this time I was prepared, and fooled every rise I covered with it - I called it the 'Bulbous Gnat'.

'Bugs'. (Page 166 / 172)

For the approach with the 'Bugs' I do have my favourite patterns and are the ones that I use most of the time with this method of angling. It may be prudent to explain at this stage that these 'Bugs' are tied using different weights for different depths of water and are frequently changed from pool to pool or sometimes within different areas of the same pool, if I am not getting down and feel the river bed then the fly is changed to ensure that I do. Some of the patterns are imitative of the natural and others are, well, just 'bugs' that catch fish. What they actually take them for I do not know it may be that it hits them on the nose or comes too close for comfort that they grab at them. Whatever, they work.

My favourites are the **'Pinky' 'Semtex' 'Bobesh' 'Cased Caddis' 'Brown and Yellow Woven',** together with a variety of Gold, Black, Copper, beaded creations. They are dressed using varying sizes of beads to suit depth and size of the hook in double tungsten plus lead, single tungsten plus lead, tungsten and the normal beads with varying body colour and varying degrees of lead added. Whilst some might frown on this and require accurate details of dressings, it may not necessarily be the correct recipe, provided that the creation gets down quickly and fishes in the manner that is attractive. I personally believe it is the profile of that dressing and its presentation that is most important. Get them down to the fish and present them in the correct manner and you will get to grips with them.

The first time I saw this 'bugging' method was when I watched the Polish gentleman fishing in the World Championship on the River Dee – as mentioned above. I saw the patterns he used which gave me an indication of what was required. It took a fair while for me to learn the 'Shuttle weave' required to produce the fly, but I had one I could work off relative to weight and profile. Sourcing the material used to create this 'bug' was not easy, I have never seen this material on sale through 'Fishing Tackle / Fly tying sales outlets' and it was whilst on a visit to a 'haberdasher' warehouse that I found my supply, it was a basket full of reels containing hundreds of yards of the stuff in varying colours - an end of production run material obviously purchased en bloc from some sewing factory. At fifty pence a reel, I was like a kid in a sweet shop. It is actually 'Polypropylene', not the shiny material but the dull looking one. When you catch hold of it you will notice that there is a very tiny stretch factor in it and if you examine it closely you will see that each of the thousands of fibres in the strand is crinkle-like and not flat and straight in the fibre. This makes it easier to create accurate patterning in the weave. These reels come in differing thickness and for some colours there was a need to double or triplicate the length of materials to get the right density.

Through trial and error at the weaving game I learnt that the secret of a good steady weave pattern could only be achieved if the under body was correct in the first place. To do this, place hook in the vice, lay on the desired amount of lead wire to weight your bug, this lead should be near the eye end of the hook leaving about 1/16" between the lead and hook eye, and only about three quarters of the way down the hook shank towards the bend. The reason for this is that you need to taper the body in towards the tail. Tie in your polypropylene yarn and build the body up tight in a cigar shape to a tapering tail, making sure that it lies smoothly with no dips and bumps in it. Pull it tight in the winding and make sure that the yarn spreads out flat to achieve this. I always use the same coloured material as I intend to weave across the back of the particular pattern Once this has been established you can angle your vice and tie in your two colours of polypropylene and create your weave right through to near the eye, checking that each weave follows the same line to the previous. Remember practice makes perfect and details of how to achieve differing weave patterns are already well published. You can use any colour you choose in your patterns, the darker colour should always be on the back of the fly.

The Brown and Yellow woven bug is a favourite and is great in the warmer months for trout and grayling. I mainly use it on the point in lower water conditions or one dropper up from the point sometimes when I need a heavyweight to get the business end down. It certainly gets a swim every outing without fail

'Semtex' and 'Bobesh' are Czech nymphs, I have had the pleasure of the company of some great anglers from the Czech Republic over the years and watched closely the methods they used to create their offerings I can assure you that they are very particular about the profile of the finished article.

'Semtex' is obviously named so due to its devastating results wherever it is fished. It was Jaromir Sraam and Martin Musil that introduced me to this pattern to copy the Hydropsyche larvae, the free swimming sedge, the one the one that does not build a house to live in. That larvae and the Rhyacophelia are good swimmers and dart about weed beds and mossy stones attacking and devouring smaller morsels. To see for yourselves catch one and put it in a bowl of water with some smaller aquatics and watch the chase and capture, they are quite vicious and also a great trout and grayling food.

The **'Czech nymph', 'Semtex'.** When I saw this pattern being dressed for the first time I was glued to the spot watching every turn of thread and positioning of the materials. A size 8 'Admiral' curved shank hook was placed in the vice and the square lead wire wound on over the apex of the bend - about twenty turns of it which covered the hook shank from near the eye over the apex and half way down towards the bend. This was over-wrapped with the tying thread to secure it in position - the amount of thread used being minimally. only enough to cover over the lead. This keeps it thin in profile and shaped at each end of the lead to taper into the hook shank. The thread was then taken forward along the hook shank nearly to the bend, where a piece of 3lb nylon about 12" in length was trapped in. Two turns of thread secured it and the next material was selected from a sheet of thin rubber - shiny on one side and dull on the other, dyed in a light brown shade. A strip about 2" long was cut and trimmed to shape in a triangle fashion along its entire length, from about quarter of an inch to about a sixteenth of an inch at the point. The rubber was laid centrally and over the top of the hook shank by the tip and tied in with two turns over towards the hook bend, with the shiny side of the material showing up.

Alongside the last turn of thread hanging off the hook shank on the bobbin there was then placed a fine flat piece of gold tinsel and this trapped in now back towards the hook eye with one turn of thread - no bulk, super slim.

A dubbing loop was then created about four to five inches in length and a dubbing spinner applied to the loop. A Hare's mask was combed with a small metal rake and the combings teased out and placed on the table. The combings from different areas of the mask were mixed using the shading within the combings from light to dark in the length of the collective dubbing arranged. With wetted finger the dubbing was picked up easily and tightened into the dubbing loop and spun, hardly any falling out and producing a very fine and secure dubbing rope. The thread was taken over in open turns along the hook shank to the hook eye and left hanging on the bobbin. The dubbing rope was then wound on over the hook shank in close even turns through to the thorax area with the lighter shading at the tip and the darker shading in the thorax. There was a slight build up of dubbing towards and in the thorax, to create a slight taper.

There was no surplus in the dubbing rope as practice had led to knowing exactly the length required when it was formed. The fine gold tinsel was then wound on in open turns to the thorax, trapped in with the tying thread and trimmed off. It pays to half hitch each separate material for security when working on a curved shank hook, the thread does tend to slip off at a crucial moment.

JaJa then took an old tooth brush that had been trimmed down and brushed the hare's ear rope in downward strokes on each side of the hook. He was very meticulous about this, using the dubbing needle too to remove trapped hairs from underneath the gold rib on both sides. The rubber back was then pulled across and over the back of the body of the nymph and positioned centrally along its length so that there was an equal amount showing to each side of the hook shank. This was tightened and tied in with the tying thread, two or three turns and a half hitch to secure.

The nylon was then brought in open turns from the hook bend through to the thorax, creating segments in the body, the turns of the nylon becoming wider towards the thorax. This was trapped in with the tying thread and the surplus trimmed before building up a small neat head and whip finished. A black permanent marker pen was used on the rubber - each side and over the back on the last two segments created with the nylon. JaJa also put some spots along the entire length on the rubber, tiny dots, just visible. Using a small pair of flat smooth nosed pliers he went along the entire body from above squeezing gently to shape the lead to profile a ridged effect along and above the apex of the hook bend through to the thorax. To finish he varnished the head and over the black coloured thorax area. I can still visualise it, perfection and very 'Buggy'.

'Bobesh' translated is 'Little Boy' and this pattern also follows a similar style in makeup to the 'Semtex' with colour variations. Why call it 'Little Boy'? Well the Czech lads use the term broadly when someone asks them what they have caught their fish on, 'Bobesh' is the pet reply, thereby cleverly giving the type of fly but not the exact pattern - they wink, nod, and laugh to each other. Not that they should be worried about showing the exact fly as they are far superior in skills in the 'Bugging' methods than most. Competitively I believe that Jaromir Sraam called by his friends 'JaJa' has been in the world championship winning Czech team on more than one occasion, and in the Silver or Bronze medal position several times and that clearly emphasises his capabilities with this and other methods.

The **'Bobesh'** is tied in the same manner but with different coloured bodies of fine dubbing. It can have different colours of rubber back plus the inclusion of fluorescent materials of various colours either red, yellow or green in the tail under the rubber back. A variation would sport a slim longish built head out of pearly tinsel. The list is never ending, but the method of producing it is essentially identical with the dressing style of the 'Semtex' ending, but the method of producing it is essentially identical with the dressing style of the 'Semtex'.

The **'Cased Caddis'** or **'Peeping Caddis'** is a very good point to use on a bug cast, I vary the size of mine from 14 to 8 on long shank hooks and of late I use the barbless keel hooks. They fish with the hook point up and snag-up on the river bed much less frequently. It's an easy fly to tie. First I put on a tungsten bead followed by a double layer of lead wire. At the tail end I use a small piece of emerald green tag with legs each side made of the butt end of plucked pheasant tail fibres, trimmed to shape. The rest of the fly is easy - a dubbing rope of squirrel fur wound on over the lead up to the black tungsten bead and tied in - that's it. Can be deadly.

'Pinky'! what a bug this is, it takes trout and grayling and I fish it throughout the year. The original is dressed based on a 'Czech nymph' style in sizes 10,12,14. and moved about on the cast to suit the day and water pressure. Clear rubber is used for the back and pearly rib over a light pink soft synthetic fibre. Its variant is different and is created with a gold tungsten bead at the head, sizes vary, followed by lead wire to the apex of the bend of a curved shank hook. The lead is covered over with white tying thread and then at the tip an eight inch piece of pearly tinsel is trapped in, not the ordinary one, the orange coloured one. If you stretch this 'Orange' coloured pearly tinsel, it goes a purple colour and finer in width. When this is wound on over the white thread in overlapping turns back to the gold bead, it shows up pink. Tie in at the bead and varnish the body to strengthen. When it is dry, create a small dubbing loop by splitting the tying thread and tease in some cut squirrel fur, short in fibre. Spin this into the rope and then create your whip finish of this rope in front of the bead. Again - a great 'Bug'.

That covers the 'Flies' and 'Bugs' that are my favourite patterns, based on catch returns over the past ten years. All that remains now is the 'Mini Lures'. These represent small fish in shape and I favour a very thin Alexandra type dressing, sporting a silver body, red tail, black hackle and over laid with a close wing of Peacock sword feathers. Hooks are size 12 and 14 long shank hook. Keep the dressing sparse. I use it on a short leader about 3' in length of 6lb to 8lb in strength. This is tedious fishing and quite hard work but sometimes very rewarding and must not be ignored – reminding me of fishing the quill minnow in my youth.

The Lake and Resevoir Flies

There are thousands of flies on the market in various guises and dressed from various materials. How on earth would one go about to select a reasonable number to address most eventualities that are encountered. One thing for certain when you tie that fly on your leader, you must fish it with the confidence. If you are not confident then select another.

My collection and array of flies began very many years ago, firstly by purchasing and also begging a few from fellow anglers when in my youth. I dress all my own these days, and have done for very many years now. I try to develop something new all the time in my mind. At each sitting with the fly-tying vice I put these ideas to the test. If it looks good, then it will have a wetting at some stage, if it works I will develop it further again, in the mind initially and put the finishing touches onto it later. From a lifetime of varying experiences with the flies I have some that hold a special place in my mind.

My favourite Lake and Reservoir dry patterns include, 'Hoppers', in Olive, Black and Orange, 'F Fly' in Olive and Black and a 'Shuttlecock' in Olive, Black, creamy white, and stripped peacock herl. In season the 'Mayfly Emerger', 'Coch-y-Bonddu', 'Heather Fly', 'Weevil', 'Cow Dung', 'Daddy', 'Bibio', never fail me and cover most eventualities. These flies range in sizes from 10 to 22 on the 'Shuttlecock' to copy a hatching caenis, naturally I taper down to 4lb with the caenis and small patterns, so that I can get the nylon through the eye of the small hooks. (Page 187 - 198)

The nymphs I dress on size 10 and 12 heavyweight hooks in Olive, Black, Claret with orange cheeks thereon. Just very simple patterns, I have a favourite nymph pattern formed out of peacock herl and pearly tinsel - another very simple but effective dressing, using black, olive and claret tying thread, to change the colour slightly. It was my friend Chris Nunn that gave me one to try, Chris used the pattern to good effect on Corrib and on his home water, Bewl Reservoir in Kent. (Page 194)

John Ifor Thomas had studied closely the insects hatching in Llyn Coron and Llyn Alaw on Anglesey. One of them, the Midge, was observed coming back in the evening to lay its eggs. John knew that the body of the ascending nymph when viewed in sunlight displayed an array of colours. His original pattern was tied using Coch y Bonddu hen hackle fibres for the tail and then a piece of Christmas decoration trapped and wound on the hook shank and held down with some superglue. The hackle was Coch y Bonddu and the wing folded starling secondary feather. (Page 195)

This fly caught trout everywhere he went and the house's supply of the Christmas decoration became quite scarce! I knew the colours well that he used and set about many years later to try and achieve a similar decoration, but to no avail. The decoration used initially had been a multicoloured rope, having spoken to John about this he suggested twisting some Lurex Tinsel of the appropriate colours together and tying this onto the hook with the aid of superglue. I played with this for a while but did not get it right until one day I was unravelling a piece of string and it dawned on me that it was twisted in one direction and all the threads then twisted together. So I set about this with Lurex tinsel and after playing with this for a while and by adding extra strands of two of the colours, I arrived at a rope that was tighter than the original and which showed uniform colours, I could by adding more turns make the rope very tight and fine. The fly worked well and still serves me well on a pulled wet fly cast. Since this fly is a must in my Lakes box I shall detail for you how the rope is formed, although today the colours that John and I used I developed into a dubbing material, much easier to tie and just as effective. It is the 'Peacock Sword Flashbright Blend' Lureflash do it.

However, Stick a 4" piece of sellotape on the table in front of you and another 12" away from it, placed vertically from you. You will need a spool of Green / Copper / Blue / Red, Lurex tinsel. Take off the spools, two pieces of green and two pieces of red, one of blue and one of copper - all about 14" long. Place them Green, Red, Blue, Green, Red, Copper all about ¼"apart under the sellotape on your left hand side, trapping them in about ½" from the end, leaving the rest trailing over towards the other sellotape piece. Between finger and thumb, roll one strand of the tinsel away from you it's not easy initially until it starts to twist. Be careful not to lose your grip on this - you can prevent it by using the finger and thumb of the other hand and then resetting for further twist, all clockwise and away from you. When the single colour is twisted up to a fine even line pull across and trap under the sellotape on the opposite side. Follow the same procedure until all of the strands are similarly twisted and trapped in parallel lines across the table in front of you.

From the furthest point away from you, under your right hand, peel the sellotape off the table slowly, twisting it again underneath the sticky side on the inside as you peel it off until you have all of it off the table and in a roll. Keep twisting it clockwise and watch the rope form. When you have twisted all the strands together and, they are uniform in colour pattern, put the finger of your left hand down on top of the rope centrally in the length and fold the right hand over taking the sellotape down to meet the other piece of sellotape stuck on the table. Then release your hold on the centre of the rope, this will then spring and twist together. Peel the other piece of sellotape off the table folding it and rolling it sticky side over the rolled piece of sellotape. Roll clockwise as you do, to keep the rope together, the piece of rope will be about 5" to 6" long and enough to dress the body on two flies, fiddly but good. I have just lost the will to live!!!

You can put a dab of superglue if you wish on the hook shank before winding on as this will aid the strength. The fly was aptly named the 'John Ifor', and whilst I am thinking about the name, I recall some years later catching a story on the televised news one evening and seeing a number of army tanks heading into battle in some distant country. I noticed one of the tanks with 'IFOR' painted on the side, my immediate thought was, that's odd, but fair play to him, the soldier within was obviously welsh, and had painted his name on the side of the tank in case it was televised so that his mother would know which tank he was in…. silly fool that I am… it was some months later when I realised what it meant, don't tell anyone will you. If some of you go "Uhhh!" Then you know, I won't feel so bad. International Forces Overseas Regiment.

The favourite flies for Llyn Alaw were the 'John Ifor' and the 'Colonel Dowman' (Page 195 /196) Sometimes the 'Mallard and Claret' would do well in that calm weather, but with a little chop the old favourite the 'Haul a Gwynt' would take top dropper position on a three fly cast. Whilst I have hoards of flies, thousands of variants of old established patterns some sporting new materials and the like, to suit any condition or circumstance I may come across, those I have selected for you here are still my favourites.

BABY SUNFLY SIZE 12 TO 18

(Page 161)

PARALOOP SUNFLY VARIANT SIZE 14 / 16

EMERGING SEDGE SIZE 12 AND 14
(Page 162)

IRON BLUE DUN SIZE 16
(Page 163)

IRON BLUE "F" FLY SIZE 16
(Page 163)

IRON BLUE "F" FLY (MOLE FUR) SIZE 16
(Page 163)

CUL DE CANON SIZE 16
(Page 91 / 163)

LARGE DARK OLIVE SIZE 14
(Page 163)

STRIPPED PEACOCK HERL OLIVE SIZE 14 / 16
(Page 163)

CUL - DE - CANON MK 2 SIZE 16
(Page 164)

CUL - DE CANON SIGHT FLY SIZE 14
(Page 164)

THE RAT SIZE 14 AND 16
(Page 164)

KILNKHAMMER OLIVE AND SIGHT INDICATOR
FOR SMALLER / LIGHTER NYMPHS (Page 164)

PHEASANT TAIL SIZE 14 / 16 / 18 / 20
(Page 165)

BULBOUS GNAT SIZE 18
(Page 165)

PINKY SIZE 10 / 12
(Page 166 - 172)

BOBESH SIZE 10 / 12
(Page 166 - 172)

SEMTEX SIZE 10 / 12
(Page 166 - 172)

PEEPING CADDIS SIZE 10 / 12
(Page 166 - 172)

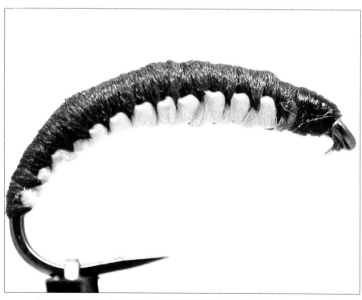

BROWN AND YELLOW WOVEN SIZE 8 / 10 / 12
(Page 166 - 172)

"F" FLY BLACK
(Page 173 - 176)

BLACK SHUTTLECOCK SIZE 12 TO 22
(Page 173 - 176)

OLIVE SHUTTLECOCK SIZE 12 TO 22
(Page 173 - 176)

WHITE AND CREAM SHUTLECOCK SIZE 22 / 24
(Page 173 - 176)

YELLOW MAYFLY EMERGER SIZE 10 LONG SHANK
(Page 173 - 176)

OLIVE MAYFLY EMERGER SIZE 10 LONG SHANK
(Page 173 - 176)

COCH - Y - BONDDU BEETLE SIZE 12
(Page 173 - 176)

HEATHER FLY SIZE 12
(Page 173 - 176)

WEEVIL BEETLE SIZE 16
(Page 173 - 176)

COW DUNG SIZE 14
(Page 173 - 176)

DADDY LONGLEGS SIZE 12
(Page 173 - 176)

BIBIO SHUTTLECOCK SIZE 12 / 14
(Page 173 - 176)

BLACK NYMPH SIZE 12 TO 20
(Page 173)

OLIVE NYMPH SIZES 12 TO 20
(Page 173)

CLARET NYMPH SIZE 8 / 10 / 12
(Page 173)

PEACOCK HERL NYMPH 8 / 10 / 12
(Page 173)

JOHN IFOR FLY SIZE 12
(Page 174)

COLONEL DOWMAN SIZE 12
(Page 176)

MALLARD AND CLARET 12 /14 /16
(Page 44 / 176)

HAUL A GWYNT (SUN AND WIND) SIZE 12
(Page 44 / 176)

HAGVAR SIZE 12
(Page 78)

YORK SPECIAL SIZE 12
(Page 78)

Y FELAN FACH (LITTLE YELLOW ONE) SIZE 12
(Page 75)

GOLD INVICTA SIZE 12
(Page 78)

FISH FRY LURE SIZE 10 LONG SHANK
(Page 172)

MALLARD BLUE AND SILVER SIZE 8 LONG SHANK
(Page 152)

MALLARD BLUE AND SILVER SIZE 8
(Page 135)

MALARD AND CLARET SIZE 8
(Page 135)

BLACK AND SILVER TUBE 3"
(Page 152)

DOVEY BLACK AND ORANGE SIZE 6
(Page 152)

SURFACE LURE 3" LONG
(Page 141)

CASCADE SINGLE SIZE 4
(Page 210)

CASCADE TREBLE SIZE 12 AND 14
(Page 210)

CURRY'S RED VARIANT SIZE 10 /12 / 14
(Page 210)

CORFF MELYN BUDYR (DIRTY YELLOW BODY)
SIZE 6 AND 8 (Page 149) (Page 210 / 211)

COCH - Y - BONDDU SIZE 6 AND 8 FOR SALMON AND
SEATROUT SIZE 10 / 12 / 14 FOR TROUT (Page 78, 149, 210)

IAR GOCH (RED HEN) SIZE 6 AND 8
(Page 14 / 210 / 211)

LLWYD YR WYDD (GREY GOOSE) SIZE 6
(Page 210)

WILLIE GUN WADDINGTON 3"
(Page 210)

CASCADE LONG SHANK TREBLE SIZE 12
(Page 210)

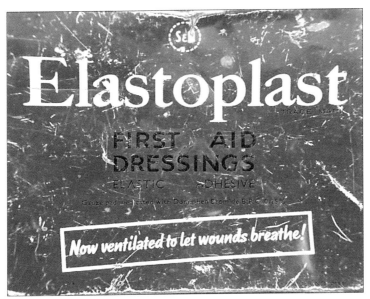

MY FATHER'S LIGHTWEIGHT FLY BOX
(Page 208)

THE CONTENTS
(Page 208)

My favourite Salmon Flies

Delving into my father's fishing bag and Salmon Fly Box at a young age and inspecting the contents in fine detail created a sense of connection to the river and to the king of fish – the salmon. Magical memories of salmo salar leaping high and attempting to throw the hook to secure its freedom. Long winter nights flew by, and that painful child yearning-longing for a time of salmon angling forays to come again quickly helped pass the months away from the river.

Constant questioning about each pattern, "Why this one?", "Dad, what's it called?", "What bird is that feather off?", could have been awfully pressing on him, but he never once faltered from answering in one way or another, sometimes resulting in a story from the past, of experiences he had encountered. It was like music to my ears and I was captivated by such tales. There always came a time however at each of these occasions when he would tell me to put the flies away and I would do so, reluctantly.

Whilst not realising it at the time, my knowledge of 'Salmon Flies', and the conditions under which each was used, was expanding. Whilst there was an array of patterns in Dad's box, only a small selection of these were used and re used time and again the season through. Each pattern in that box had some history attached to it. Success at the top of the list through to some one else's favourite pattern, given to him as a 'sure fire killer' of fish. These possibly never saw the water on his line. He always travelled light as he walked a long way in search of the Salmon and Seatrout, he had an array of flies in an Elastoplast tin.

Each time the tying vice and feather box came out of the sideboard and onto the cleared kitchen table, I was there peering at the creation of yet another addition to the array in the Fly box. I watched, mesmerised, each twist of feather and fibre against each turn of thread on the hook shank. Each time it would be an additional 'favourite' pattern, no new development of that pattern.

Just perfecting the style in which the feathers and silk portrayed themselves on the hook shank.

Bringing these thoughts forward to the present day and my array of Salmon flies, nothing has really changed in the fact that I also now have my own 'favourites' suited to conditions and location at which they are used.

Whilst I have many boxes of all kinds of patterns through from the built wing specials of days gone by to the modern hair winged, and shrimp style patterns of today, seldom do I find the need to change my 'favourite' patterns. I have been known to give some non favourite, but nice looking fly, a swim, when things are slow only to change back to another favourite in quick time whilst actually fishing. This tendency in me is possibly created through experience of success and the confidence that comes with it, for if you fish with confidence in the pattern of fly chosen then the chances are that you will eventually succeed.

To evaluate one pattern against another, is playing in an area that could just add to confusion so I will leave that well alone and tell you only what I have found to be successful in my experiences. I suppose that, if reviewed on a survey basis among all Salmon anglers, one could reach a conclusion as to why so few flies attach themselves to each individual angler, and maybe the reason for this, is that it is the angler that is caught by the fly?, perhaps that is true?, but for me it is mainly down to personal preferences based on successful experiences. My favourite patterns, possibly with the addition of a twist or other of some material through personal choice to the original dressings of the known patterns, well, the ones that have caught me most fish, are:

The 'Shrimp', and variations of original tyings, gold body, silver body in, Hot Orange and Ruby Red , 'Cascade', 'Willie Gunn', all on sizes 8, 10, 12, 14 Viking treble hooks. Some have a light underbody of lead to aid the presentation aspect in varying water heights, fished off a floating or sink tip line. These flies are for use in high and dropping water conditions on the larger rivers that I fish with the double handed rod.

For really heavy water, cold conditions and fast sink line techniques I use the 'Willie Gunn' and 'Cascade' tied on Aluminium Tubes and also Waddington shanks, both standard and gold body version, 1.5" to 2.5" long.

In the Autumn I use a traditional salmon single size 2 hook with a double 18lb leafguard to protect the hook point with a lead wire underbody. These days a 'Cascade' is a favourite, now that is a relatively new created pattern, so possibly the 'fly caught me'.

For the spate rivers I use a Llwyd-yr-Wydd (Grey Goose) on double salmon irons in size 8 , 10, 12. Coch-y-Bonddu, Iar Goch (Red Hen), Corff Melyn Budr, (Dirty Yellow Body) and Bibio in size 6 and 8 bronze hooks for the dropper position on a high and dropping river.

On the larger rivers when using a single handed rod I use the Black and Silver on the point and a Peter Ross on the dropper especially if there is only a small rise in the water.

Let me explain the Welsh named patterns. 'Llwyd-yr-Wydd' is from the stable of Dr Shelton Roberts, a doctor whose Surgery was at Pen-y-Groes, not far from the River Dwyfawr - that he fished many years ago. 'Coch-y-Bonddu' should need no introduction and is a well established trout pattern for when the beetle appears in droves in June. This, tied in wet fashion on larger hooks works well for Salmon and Seatrout in spate rivers.

'Iar Goch' is the pattern given to my father by the elderly farmer who lived at Ty Cerrig in the upper reaches of the River Dwyfawr, mentioned in an earlier chapter. 'Corff Melyn Budr' is an interesting pattern with origins. I recall clearly how my father went about achieving the body colours He used the wool from an old army sock, the light mottled grey wool, together with yellow lichen he scraped into a paper bag with a penknife off the roof of an old cowshed, not far from my home. A pan with a little water was placed on the electric ring and brought to boil before the wool and lichen were added. These would boil away for some time and he would check every so often to make sure that the pan had not boiled dry. To integrate the resulting colour into the wool he would add vinegar and I seem to recall that my mother was none to pleased about this practice for it stank the house out and it would linger so she said for days. One thing for certain the resultant colour was a sure catcher of fish, or was it a sure fire catcher of 'boys' and 'men' alike? (Page 204 / 205).

My favourite Brown Trout River

Since 1999 I have been a regular visitor to the River Liffey in County Kildare, and during the whole of my fishing life I have never experienced any dry fly, river fishing of this quality the river is stuffed with free rising trout. I suppose that at one time most rivers were once of the same stamp as the Liffey, but sadly are now a shadow of their former selves. Not the Liffey however!

Whilst present development in the Newbridge area and the explosion in the population gives cause for concern over the future of this great river, there is one thing that really stands out and is possibly the key to the prolific fly life that exists there. It is, racehorse country with a sprinkling of small farms and very few sheep and cattle. To keep livestock from the river and vice versa, it is, in the main, fenced off twenty yards back from each bank and is completely wild and overgrown. Thus it has a truly great habitat. No sheep dip, no great quantities of fertilizer thrown onto the fields, little bank erosion all make a difference. You can even pick up freshwater mussels three to four inches long and once I waded through a pool with my net hanging behind me and when I came out to my amazement there were two crayfish in it. The aquatic environment is very healthy and lends itself to producing large quantities of fast growing and free-rising wild brown trout..

My introduction to the Liffey came in the way of an International Fly fishing Match in 1999. I was in the Welsh Team, having been successful in 1998 on the River Tweed. I didn't know what to expect really, although the enquiries that I had made showed that the River was very prolific. I was to find

212

out in the first outing on this river how prolific it really was as I proceeded to take trout after trout with a dry fly on a long pool right in the middle of the town of Newbridge. Since 1999 I have been fishing the river on a regular basis at certain times of the year. Even if the fishing is poor on these visits it supercedes anywhere else I have had the pleasure of fishing at for wild brown trout. To say that the fishing is phenomenal is an understatement.

Hatches are present from the first day of the season till the last and the trout in the main are looking up for most if not all of the time. The Large Dark Olive starts mixed in with millions of chironomids, followed by the Iron Blue, which in broken weather can occur throughout the season. The Blue Winged Olive hatch is amazing and I can recall a cold snap in June one year when I visited and in the evenings the lit up shop windows in Newbridge were plastered with Blue Wings coming off the river. I've never seen the like of it before or after. There was some heat coming from the shops and the Blue wings rested on the glass windows. Sedges together with the crustaceans and minnows also provide plentiful supply of food for the trout. I have observed minnows in shallow water, 2" deep right up against the bank on a gravel bed, being herded there by two or three trout 12" to 14" long. Then all of the sudden one made a dart for the minnows almost beaching itself before splashing back into depth with its meal. (Page 102) a lucky shot of the incident.

The fish in the Newbridge area average about 9" and some go to 12" or more with large numbers in the 6" to 8" bracket. As you move upstream the fish get smaller but more prolific whereas as you move downstream, less fish but larger - average 12" and some up to 5lb! A number of these are stalked by the 'In the know regulars' each year and returned. They are very wary, but catchable - all exciting stuff and just mind blowing dry fly fishing.

Whilst there are some very deep slow moving pools that you are unable to wade through, for most of the fishery you are able to walk upstream crossing from one bank to the other fishing between the weeds and into pots and glide upon glide of crystal clear water 18" to 3' deep. The glides are separated by what are termed 'sharps', fast riffley water - all fish holding areas. Willow trees grow out of the river in places and others have fallen in creating great habitat both for the trout and insects alike. Gravel areas and silted areas run through pods of ranunculus weeds, making for varied and very interesting presentation problems. What amazes me most is the fact that you can walk up through a section, fishing away and encounter nothing - you'd think the place was devoid of fish and then the hatch comes on and with it a serious rise. You turn around and walk back through the same area and catch trout after trout, on the downstream dry - they do not spook easily when the hatch is on.

A good time to start, I make the pilgrimage now on an annual basis, is St Patricks Day or as they say in Ireland 'Paddy's Day' - the 17th March. Large dark olives will be present as will tiny chironomids and the trout are looking up. For some period during the day there will be a rise of fish so one must search in the areas where one sees the froth bubbles floating downstream. Some anglers call them 'suds', fish the 'suds' they say and you will be in with a chance.

I recall one very cold 'Paddy's Day', hands almost frozen and fishing with nymphs with little effect when I experienced an almighty hail storm. The whole place was white and at one stage during the storm such was the force and ferocity of the hail hitting the rod that I put it in the water in case it was damaged. Immediately after the storm passed the whole river erupted and fish rose everywhere to a hatch of Olives. For whatever reason the hail brought on a huge hatch and the fish obliged - an experience I'll never forget.

Other times when very warm, fishing can be very tricky because although the fish will rise steadily they can become preoccupied with a certain morsel or a certain stage in the hatching progress. This calls for a careful approach, identification of what is being taken and a quick change of fly, tactics and presentation. This is all good stuff in that it hones the skills and fine tunes your mind towards successful methods. This kind of fishing skill cannot really be taught to anyone - it is more self taught and based on observation, experience and many hours of failing miserably.

Fishing with the nymph in front of the dry is also very good on the Liffey and the more difficult trout seem to succumb to this method. As you wade along you will soon learn that behind each weed bed lies a pot that the water has created in the gravel. It may only be 18" deep but it will hold a number of fish and a cast aimed to the side of and level with the weed will see the nymph drift into the pot and a take is sure to follow if you get the presentation right. It must be dead drift fashion and provided you are in the blind spot behind the fish, he will have a go at it.

These pots are also found in the very shallow water in between pools. You may be wading only to your ankles in water but in front of you there will be a pot or several of them 12" to 18" deep. Look for them , they all hold or are potential fish lies and are easily fished although a bit difficult with a dry because of the drag problems associated with an upstream approach and the water movement over the pot. On a downstream dry however, with a properly executed parachute or slack line cast, they are fishable.

You may think that in the low clear water the trout would easily spook, but for some reason on the Liffey, when they are on the feed, they seem oblivious to your approach until you are right on top of them. By then it should be too late anyway, as you will have made your presentation, hopefully successfully.

If there is no noticeable hatch, trout still appear on the surface and dimple all day long on the flats. These fish are not easily approached or caught and can be put down with line flash and the like. They are feeding on minute insects, usually very small chironomids, termed on the Liffey, the 'Black stuff'. It can prove to be very interesting fishing because if you target an individual fish and you spook him, wait a while and he'll come back on the feed. Then you can cover him again from a different angle. It does work and you get a real sense of achievement that you have fooled it when it actually sips down your offering - it's a lovely sound too to add to the excitement – a soft Irish brogue version of 'sip'.

Other Species on Fly

If you have never had a go I urge you to make an appointment with this one. 'Bonefish', magical environment, warm , relaxing, stunning colourful scenery and tons of fish, whatever you do if it's your first time, go with a 'Guide' their assistance will make your holiday.

My first trip was to 'Great Exuma' in the Bahamas, staying at the 'Peace and Plenty' on this wonderful Island. Having first stopped off in Miami a first on American soil too, the two hour flight to Exuma in a twin engine twenty seater gives an insight into the vast amount of flats available - blue and green colours like you have never seen before.

On arrival at the Peace and Plenty and having registered in the reception I walked through into our room, which over looked the swimming pool. Having dumped the bags, my wife sent me packing onto the beach whilst she enjoyed her first Bahamas special Cocktail alongside the pool. Not more than twenty steps from our room I was on the beach and strolling along, looking into the crystal clear water, I stopped in my tracks and wondered whether all the reading I had done and picture's I had observed in magazines were playing tricks with my eyes and mind. Not more than five yards away from me in about twelve inches of water lay this fish, its fins bristling away, basking in the sun. The next step I took saw it disappear in a cloud of sand as it tore off at alarming pace. I was not dreaming at all I had just seen my first Bonefish.

I returned excitedly to the pool side to relate what I had seen and by this time my friend Terry Morgan had appeared. In spite of the laughter of our wives at our boyish excitement, we were kitted up and away onto the beach in no time. Terry went in one direction and I in the opposite. The water was lovely and warm, just like bath water and the area in front of the hotel was part of a small bay with two peninsula points almost meeting each other forming a channel into the open water beyond. As I made my way along I noticed some coloured water ahead and out towards the middle of the bay. I had read about the 'Bonefish' muddying the water in search of crabs and the like and was not sure whether this was such a situation. The first cast of the fly into the area met with a solid take and a reel screeching run into the distance. I was amazed again at the speed and ferocity of the fish which when brought to hand some minutes later barely made two pounds. (Page 104) I 'd had my first taste of 'Bonefish' with my first cast and wow it was brilliant. This was followed by another but it threw the hook. I then I returned to the pool area to join the ladies and sample the local beverage before dinner and bed. Terry had two or three that afternoon but he'd walked round the bay to the peninsula and back. I needed no rocking to sleep that evening.

The next morning we were picked up at the front door by our guide and were driven some miles to the Bonefish Lodge where the boats were waiting. We shared a guide and were taken on an amazing run through various channels within mangroves that opened out into large flats as far as the eye could see. It was great travelling in the skiff, lovely and cool, but very hot when you stopped and waded along. The guide could spot the fish at a great distance away and I found this very difficult to start with. He would tell you when and where to cast to and more often than not he was spot on.

Sharing the flats we visited were Lemon Sharks and large Stingrays, some Barracuda and small baitfish of all kinds, magical to see. I was wary of the sharks who would bask in the sun in barely two feet of water with the dorsal fin breaking the surface. The guide would walk along pick up a handful of wet coral and sand and throw it in the direction of the shark and they would slink away quietly. He told us that they were not dangerous, but I had my doubts - a shark is a shark is a shark.

We continued stalking Bonefish off the skiff taking it in turns catching a few up to five pounds in weight. A whole new chapter had opened up in my fishing exploits and I was enjoying every minute of it. I recall that during the week we also found some muddying bonefish way out over deeper water as the tide sent us from flat to flat and we took nineteen between us off one muddy area - exceptional sport.

Such was the amazing scenery and colours we soaked up on a daily basis that we decided to split up one day and take our wives out so that they would see and experience this beauty also. I recall coming onto a flat and the guide telling me that we would wade down the side of a mangrove towards the rising tide because it usually held some large bonefish and was worth a try. So we left the boat but my wife on seeing the first shark in the distance was back in the skiff in seconds.

The guide and I waded along quietly and encountered some bonefish but could do nothing with them for some reason. By this time the tide was rising fast and I was up to my thighs in the water when he suggested I waited there whilst he returned for the skiff. He pointed to me the area that the bonefish would approach from and left me there - a few hundred yards from the skiff . Then I noticed the flash of a tail glinting in the sun as a bonefish dug into the sand after some morsel and then the wake coming towards me. I laid the cast on its nose, but unfortunately too close and spooked him. Whilst retrieving the line quickly a needle fish of about about 1.5 lb grabbed the fly and started to jump about and as I got control over him and was pulling him towards me, not more than five yards away, out of the mangrove comes a shark, possibly five feet in length with the dorsal fin slicing the surface. The needlefish panicked and took off with the shark in pursuit foolishly in that split second I held onto the fly line and the needlefish and shark circled me. The poor needle fish jumped in an attempt to escape but the shark followed and made good its lunch and disappeared back into the mangrove. When I pulled the line back in, all there was left was the needle fishes head on the fly. I have not experienced a better laxative and I was ever so pleased to see the skiff approach.

There was nothing special in the fly patterns we used at Great Exuma - the 'Crazy Charlies' and similar patterns were the best. Much is already written about these and methods from anglers who have vast experience, so I will not dwell on them here. Put 'Bonefish' down in the must do list for you will never regret it.

My only other experience of 'Bonefish' was in Tobago in the West Indies where the fish were scarcer but much larger. We had a day fishing for them on the 'Boca Reef' with a guide. It was only one flat but it was amazing as there were also small shoals of Permit there. My only encounter with one was on a crab pattern – the fish leaving the flat over the coral reef and heading into the deep water at a pace that I never imagined possible, prior to searing the line on the rough coral edge, my Hardy reel was hot to the touch when I went to wind in a hundred and fifty yards of backing and the remains of the flyline.

I did manage a 'Dorado' of about ten pounds trolling a feathered creation behind the boat over deep water on another excursion in Tobago. That was also a new experience. They pull very hard and jump very high.

On another excursion out of Barbados I managed 'King fish' again through trolling a lure at high speed past floating debris, I would estimate some 4 miles out over deep water, you could not say that was fly fishing, but it was fishing none the less.

Whilst I fish on a regular basis now for Bass, Garfish, Mackerel and Mullet around the shores of North Wales, my initial foray into the Sea fishing world was in my childhood when I accompanied my father and Uncle Sam to fish for wrasse and Pollack with peeler crab off the rocks at Porth Ysgaden, Tudweiliog on the Lleyn Peninsula. The rods used were cut down and ferruled bamboo carpet carriers with rings made out of copper wire and lashed on with treated string. This was fitted with a large wooden reel. Now I tackle these with a fast sink shooting head and various creations, difficult, but have had some success.

The peeler crab was mounted onto the size 2 hook and then secured on with copious amounts of turns of white cotton on 20lb nylon line and a large lead weight. No casting was involved - you just lowered the bait down in to the depths off the rocks. It was a really mean place to get to and you needed the stiffness of the bamboo rod to prevent the wrasse and pollack from diving into the seaweed and freeing themselves, with a fly rod it is very seldom that a good fish can be kept away from the seaweed, due to the suppleness of the rod used and the power needed to keep them above it. I have found that the method works alongside rocks where they feed, but more often than not only the smaller fish are actually brought to hand.

Ever tried roast wrasse full of sage and onion stuffing? Well it's delicious and adds to the loads of fun of catching them and preventing them from diving into the seaweed. The bonefish was a far cry from Porth Ysgaden and to even attempt a comparison is a non starter. Each have their merits and whilst the bonefish is a sporting fish, the Wrasse and Pollack was my supper.

When I very occasionally fish for cyprinids on fly, some strange looks and comments come from other anglers who are sometimes present. Well, suffice to say that the fish occur naturally in the various waters and their main diet is aquatic insects which also occur naturally. The various baits, boilies, dog biscuits that are fed to them are not natural although effective. I have nothing against anyone who sits there soaking up the atmosphere and catching fish in the way that they wish, each to his own. I have managed copious amounts of Rudd, Roach, Chub on dry fly mostly with small shuttlecock patterns of various colours, size 20 to 26, and enjoyed every minute of it, in fact I can also add that I have converted some anglers to tackling these fish on 'Fly'.

One other species I have been fortunate to catch was some 'Twaite Shad' on the River Usk in 2007, these fish a relative of the Tarpon come into fresh water to spawn, and can provide tremendous sport. They must be handled very carefully and returned to the river if you happen upon a shoal. (Page 102)

The learning curve in angling in its various guises is constant, rewarding and sometimes unexpected, long may that continue for it is on the basis of that fact alone that makes the sport so compelling and addictive.

'The Future, what is in store?'

I only wished I knew for certain, like some I could make a fortune out of it, but there we have it no one really knows with certainty, many guesses are made some based on what is termed scientific research on various subjects and whilst we all live in the hope of miracles, seldom do they reach expectations or come everyone's way.

On looking back through the memory bank of the past fifty years, relevant but almost insignificant in evolvement of time, there have been very many changes, some are alright but none I regard as very good, some awful, but there again it is only an opinion and one man's meat is another's poison so we are on a merry go round without even trying. This is not directed at any individual but at the system as I see it.

We all have our views, some of us have our say for what it's worth and more often than not dependant on the recipient of a common sense based view if it's not to the direct advantage of that individual concerned, no heed is taken and this beggars belief in the face of the continual decline we are experiencing in our rivers. Maybe they do take on board what is said and shudder, a little, but only momentarily, or maybe they do not begin to understand or they choose to ignore in order to suit present financial and performance indicated figures someone dreamed up sat behind a computer in an over populated office block with a view to get to the end of the month to pick up a fat salary cheque driven by correctness within establishments that have become paper orientated (Big deep breath) people with ashen faces not getting that double hit of the sun once from above and the reflection of it off the rivers they are supposed to be looking after for us, dragged away from reality by a plethora of unnecessary and inappropriate meetings indoors. Come to think of it why do I think I am right? ranting away like this, sat behind this desk writing this.

Well there is one thing that we can be sure of 'Nature' has her way of sorting matters out. It is a great shame that mankind does not help 'Nature' all of the time and a greater shame that some well educated and clever individuals within the society we live in have a vested interest in businesses that pay large dividends through shareholdings and profit sharing deals, the very people in the know pushing all points for financial gain irrespective of the damage to 'Nature', orientated from their gotten gains, this includes the very rivers that I am referring to. They will realise when they have to eat their £5,£10,£20 notes, that it does not taste so good after all.

We are living in a nightmare age of constant meetings where grown men and women sat opposite each other discussing and trying to agree what has gone wrong, sometimes I wonder if it involves matters that some of them do not even begin to understand. It is suspected that they know very little about the subject they are discussing or it is immaterial to them. There must be something wrong otherwise there would be no need for meetings and planning strategies, someone must have made a mess of things and in some cases paid well over a long period of time for doing just that. I agree reluctantly with scientific research for and on our rivers and the attachments that go with it provided that funding for this is sought outside the throve of the present income from Government. Back in time the 'River Boards' who were in charge upheld the statute laws to do with fisheries through enforcement of an Act of parliament well thought out for the protection of fisheries, is it not common sense that to reach sustainability within this troubled time enforcement of the statute law in full is part of what is required. What we are faced with is a depletion in this enforcement caused by that merry go round situation I describe.

I know from experience that rant from me alone will have no bearing on the situation the machinery within establishments will see to that, tut! tut!…

It is my honest opinion that what we are facing today we have faced in the past in the rolling stone mechanism of time. Ice age / Global warming, its happened before, was man blamed for it before?, that we shall never know. He is allegedly involved this time with the present high speed living we have become accustomed to, a suspect if nothing else.

Someone dreamed up an idea to steal more money off us, calling it a 'Green Tax', hey! that will get us some votes, pat on the back , tick the box jobbie. Not so long ago actually this Country was full of 'Carthorses' who possibly produced more gases towards global warming in a day... than all the vehicles put together do now in a week. 'Substantiate' that claim! "I will if you will" I rest my case, daylight robbery, nothing else.

On the other hand within establishments there are some success stories where rivers have been turned around from near extinction to sustaining a flourishing and enhancing population of Salmon, Sea trout and Trout . How has this been achieved then?, by a carefully orchestrated and concerted effort by a dedicated across the board team who have taken action, not just sat in meetings and discussed possibilities, that is how it has happened. More of that is needed and on a management level round pegs in round holes, application of the intelligent ideas.

At this moment in time I believe that whilst recognition is made of concerns that are being raised over the future of our rivers in Wales, there is not one individual ready to grasp the nettle and make the necessary wholesale moves to bring about a plan that would help to improve our rivers. Whilst some individuals do good work in localised area's, the efforts on a small scale will not bring about a sustainable growth year on year in the game fish population.

When you cover one aspect of default, cracks appear in another possibly driven by financial constraints or there isn't a box to tick, or matters are left in abeyance. Without that planned approach on a balanced front with all aspects being looked at together, I feel that the problems will continue as they are and we shall only see a barely sustainable stock for each river. This is a far cry from what I and many others my age saw and experienced in the period 1950 to 1960. On the other hand a dedicated common sense based approach with everyone pulling together and no political points to score may well enhance the situation far quicker than anyone could imagine. Is there anyone out there ready to grasp that nettle?, if so put that person in charge and lets go for it, we owe it to the future it is our duty to those who will follow us.

The marrying up of fisheries enforcement to waste disposal in the form of catching offenders 'fly tipping' and the like using the staffing level from the fisheries enforcement side to do the fly tipping side is irresponsible behaviour on behalf of Management, bordering on neglect. Management who are constantly facing criticism who married the two together depleting the fisheries enforcement staffing levels are playing with our rivers those of which were handed on into our care , our heritage and the future heritage of our children. Do these people have little or no experience of fisheries?. When the Environment Agency was given the remit of control initially I wonder if through assumption on behalf of management the funding destined for fisheries were re directed for other Environmental purposes, by non fisheries personnel who were in charge or was this a government based decision of sorts? 'We'll use this money to tackle a problem other than fisheries, we shall not tell anyone we are doing so, no one will notice, it will be fine, the public at large can see the rubbish thrown at the side of roads or in countryside area's, they can't see the decline of the fish or their food at source in the rivers'.

Responsibility for the fisheries, their maintenance development and improvement under an Act of Parliament lies solely with the Environment Agency , now then can action be imposed ? in other words we need round pegs in round holes, round pegs in square holes are noisy and ineffective, we do have a breakdown on the fisheries side.

With dwindling stocks of these very precious game fish would it not be prudent to have more fisheries enforcement staff to look after them. They should make sure that the breeding stock have a free run at the spawning sites undisturbed by poachers and other forces and also ensuring that those very streams and ditches are free of pollution and full of insect life, to give nature a fair chance at rekindling and attempting to develop what existed in the 1950's and 1960's. As responsible anglers we harvest some of the stock, but try to ensure that there are enough to reproduce. In the 1960's there were 24 fisheries enforcement officers employed to cover North Wales, now there are 8 and 'Fly-tipping' is part of their remit, leaving the rivers with a depleted form of protective cover. Sometimes this is at crucial times of the year, a scandalous strategy.

I can only wish that in the turnover of time that the situation improves and that someone puts a common sense perspective into action to help it along. I wonder and hope that in a hundred years time when someone reads this that again we shall be experiencing what I experienced in my childhood youth through to young adulthood, halcyon days or will it be the opposite?. The 21st century has a long way to go yet and for all we know there could be a big bang before the end of it.

I think we should make the most of what we have presently and try not to damage it too much in the process, don't you. Just take a moment to look around you wherever you may be.

Ask yourself these questions.

When was the last time I heard a 'Curlew' call on a summers evening?

When was the last time I saw a 'Golden Plover'?

How many snakes / hedgehogs have I seen in the past five years?

How many times have I had to wash dead insects off the screen of the car this year ?

The RSPB are very worried about the numbers of wild birds. The Anglers are worried about the declining stock of Game fish, the writing is on the wall for all to see.

Yes ! the message is clear, those very insects are the food of the young of these birds, small mammals, and the small fish in our rivers, they are all in decline. Look after the habitat and the fish will look after themselves.

Farming methods have changed, modern man and modern man methods and thinking is not all that great after all. It is unfortunately to the detriment of 'Nature', we need to re think.

Now i've had my rant and I've tried to detail where, when, how and why I have spent my life closely following the 'Angle game' in the hope that it may assist someone to develop personal skills in the future.

If you haven't guessed it already, all that remains for me to do now is to 'Just go fishing', may your lines always be tight.

Gwilym Hughes

CHAPTER INDEX

TABLE OF REFERENCE

TABLE OF REFERENCE

'HARDY FLY FISHING SCHOOL'

CONTACT

GWILYM HUGHES

ghughes2@btinternet.com

01490 412731

FOR LATEST 'UPDATES' PLEASE VISIT

www.GwilymHughes.com

'G.H.SPORTING'
FLY FISHING TUITION
GUIDED FISHING
FOR
SALMON / SEATROUT
BROWN TROUT / GRAYLING
PIKE / BASS / MULLET

CASTING TUITION
CASTING DEMONSTRATIONS

FLY DRESSING TUITION
FLY DRESSING DEMONSTRATIONS

GRAYLING FISHING SCHOOL

SMALL WATER FISHERY SCHOOL

FISHING HOLIDAYS IN WALES
ARRANGED
SHORT BREAKS
ONE - TO - ONE
SMALL - GROUP
CORPORATE EVENTS

STUCK ON AN IDEA FOR A PRESENT ?

WHAT SHALL I HAVE FOR CHRISTMAS ?
WHAT SHALL I HAVE FOR MY BIRTHDAY ?
WHAT ABOUT A

'GIFT VOUCHER'

CHECK THE WEBSITE
'UPDATED ON A REGULAR BASIS'
www.GwilymHughes.com

CHOOSE WHAT YOU WOULD
LIKE TO DO THEN ARRANGE A

'GIFT VOUCHER'

GUIDED FISHING DAY
DVD'S / CASTING TUITION

SHORT BREAK HOLIDAY...

Contact Gwilym Hughes:
ghughes2@btinternet.com

DVD Programmes

Available from 'G. H.Sporting'

www. GwilymHughes.com

Contact: Gwilym Hughes   ghughes2@btinternet.com